HBR'S 10 MUST READS

The definitive
management ideas
of the year from
Harvard Business Review.

2015

HBR's 10 Must Reads series is the definitive collection of ideas and best practices for aspiring and experienced leaders alike. These books offer essential reading selected from the pages of *Harvard Business Review* on topics critical to the success of every manager.

Titles include:

**HBR'S
10
MUST
READS**

The definitive
management ideas
of the year from
Harvard Business Review.

2015

HARVARD BUSINESS REVIEW PRESS
Boston, Massachusetts

HBR Press Quantity Sales Discounts

Harvard Business Review Press titles are available at significant quantity discounts when purchased in bulk for client gifts, sales promotions, and premiums. Special editions, including books with corporate logos, customized covers, and letters from the company or CEO printed in the front matter, as well as excerpts of existing books, can also be created in large quantities for special needs.

For details and discount information for both print and ebook formats, contact booksales@harvardbusiness.org, tel. 800-988-0886, or www.hbr.org/bulksales.

Library of Congress Cataloging-in-Publication Data

HBR's 10 must reads 2015 : the definitive management ideas of the year from Harvard business review.
   pages cm
ISBN 978-1-63369-464-4 — ISBN 978-1-63369-022-6 (ebook)
1. Management.   I. Harvard Business Review Press.   II. Harvard business review.
   HD31.H39457 2015
   658—dc23
                                                    2014046473

Contents

Putting together an issue of *Harvard Business Review* is a balancing act. We want to include the best academic thinking—and best-practice insights from organizations. New ideas—and ways to apply old ideas to new challenges. Fresh thinking about problems in the global economy—and about the problems people face every day at work.

If we get this balance right issue after issue, larger themes emerge over the course of a full year. That was certainly the case here: As we selected this group of articles, their authors almost seemed to be talking to one another. Several lines of thought stand out: An increased focus on how we spend our professional time, given that it feels (and is) ever scarcer. All the ways we find to avoid making tough choices. The inequities of 21st-century capitalism and the threats they pose. How difficult it is to move managerial ideas across geographic—and organizational—boundaries. We'll be interested to learn what additional themes emerge for readers of this collection.

We lead off with **"Beware the Next Big Thing"** in part because it offers subtle advice on how to read and apply these articles. Big-bang ideas come with their own hype machine, but Julian Birkinshaw, who studies the evolution of management ideas, says that it's never a good idea to adopt a new idea or best practice wholesale. Companies are more successful when they figure out what principles underlie the idea they want to borrow and then, if this deeper analysis suggests that it's actually relevant, experiment with adapting it to their needs.

Tarun Khanna gets at something similar in his magisterial article **"Contextual Intelligence."** Suppose you have a well-oiled, successful operating model in one country or region. Thirty years of experience with globalization has taught us that the process of applying that model to another setting is profoundly difficult. Khanna traces the experience of the German wholesaler Metro Cash & Carry as it moved from Germany into Russia, China, and then India. Ultimately it succeeded in each of those markets—but in every case, becoming profitable took years longer than expected. The speed of technological change leads us to assume that institutional, social, and economic transformations take place much faster than they actually do.

Speaking of institutional change, we were haunted this year by two uncomfortable questions: Is the concentration of power and wealth at the top of the U.S. economy hurting not just the middle class but business itself—and potentially the whole economy? And is pressure to deliver short-term performance damaging businesses' capacity to foster long-term growth? **"The Capitalist's Dilemma,"** by Clayton M. Christensen and Derek van Bever, is one in a cluster of articles that ask those questions. Corporations are sitting on unprecedented amounts of cash, the authors point out. Why, then, aren't they investing more ambitiously in innovations that could jumpstart economic growth? Christensen and van Bever argue that the metrics used by investors and executives rate investments that are focused on efficiency and incremental growth higher than those that are focused on market-creating innovations. To change our patterns of investment, we need to change the tools we use.

Roger L. Martin tackles our failure to invest ambitiously from a different perspective in **"The Big Lie of Strategic Planning."** We all know that in theory, strategy is about making choices—walking away from some opportunities and targeting others. But in practice, most companies are afraid to place big bets. They prefer to treat the annual budgeting process as their "strategic planning" moment and fail to move outside their comfort zone as a result. Signs that you're not taking strategy seriously: You have a detailed operational plan for the next one to three years. You are comfortable with the plan. The future does not terrify you. In most industries, companies can't afford that kind of complacency. Growth is an imperative, and it won't happen in the absence of ambitious, tough decisions.

Another theme that cropped up: Traditional ways of managing corporate functions are badly out-of-date. Patty McCord, formerly the chief talent officer of Netflix, wrote the irreverent **"How Netflix Reinvented HR"** with that in mind. (Actually, she and Netflix's founder, Reed Hastings, coauthored a slide deck on the topic that's been viewed millions of times on the web; we asked her to develop it into an article. That was a first for us.) Our favorite advice: Hire only people who are fully formed adults, and then treat them like adults.

Marketing, also in need of an organizational overhaul, used to muddle along successfully as a stand-alone department. Not anymore. The best marketing teams have become so intermingled with IT and analytics that they're often run by the same person, according to the authors of **"The Ultimate Marketing Machine."** But org charts are almost beside the point, because most work now gets done by fast-moving, short-lived project teams staffed by people not just from marketing but from finance, IT, and a host of other functions. (The description of how to manage project-based work is so powerful that we thought about focusing the entire article on that topic.)

Those two articles described managers who saw the need to revamp well-established managerial practices. At Google, however, most employees didn't see the point of management, period. Google's engineers, whose values permeate the company culture, tend to consider time spent supervising people as time stolen from real work. Top managers suspected they were wrong—and, Google style, they asked a group of analytics PhDs to test their hypothesis. As David A. Garvin tells the story in **"How Google Sold Its Engineers on Management,"** the analysts eventually proved that highly rated managers had lower turnover, greater productivity, happier employees, and better overall performance. The methodology was rigorous enough for the company to conclude overwhelmingly that management does matter (this was a relief to us) and that managers can take specific actions to become better at it.

HBR usually considers time management at the individual level, but this year we paid attention to organizational time. The Bain partners who wrote **"Your Scarcest Resource"** point out that the data available from Outlook and other online tools now make the amount of time we spend on various activities and tasks transparent. Among their scarier findings was that one company's weekly ExCom meeting, which eats up 7,000 direct hours a year, devours 300,000 hours when all the prep time and follow-up meetings that cascade down through other levels of the organization are included. If time is your scarcest organizational resource, you should think extremely carefully about how you spend it. (A wild guess: Less of it should be spent in meetings.)

W. Chan Kim and Renée Mauborgne looked at how categories of managers spend their time. In **"Blue Ocean Leadership"** they describe using value curves—traditionally a strategy-making tool—to study this organizational question. Here's how it worked: First the authors gathered information from frontline, middle, and senior managers' "customers"—the people who work with them—about how those managers actually spend their days. Then they gathered information about how those managers would ideally spend their time, and mapped the two data sets against each other, showing where each cohort should shift its focus. That the value-curve exercise proved so helpful in this unfamiliar setting made us wonder what other classic tools might be repurposed in this way.

Underlying both those articles is an uneasy sense that individual leaders need to do a better job of managing their own attention—and that it's increasingly difficult to do so. Daniel Goleman dives deep into emotional intelligence, neuroscience, and other disciplines in his exploration of **"The Focused Leader."** It turns out that "focus" is a gnarly concept: Different kinds of focus call on different cognitive and emotional skills, not to mention neural pathways. Goleman provides not just a fascinating tour of this terrain, but a host of practical tips for expanding awareness, developing self-restraint, and understanding your own limitations.

Time, managerial attention, and capital are all competing for the role of a company's "scarcest resource." Claudio Fernández-Aráoz introduces a fourth claimant, arguing that talent wins the contest hands down; we don't know many CEOs who would disagree. In **"21st-Century Talent Spotting"** he argues for a change in how we hire. Decades ago we hired first for strength, then for intelligence, and then for specific competencies. Indeed, intelligence and relevant experience still count for a lot, as do emotional smarts. But the best lens to look through now is *potential*. It's much harder to judge than earlier hiring criteria were (according to the author, most high-potential programs inside companies do a terrible job), but the payoff is enormous.

Some management challenges never go away (the mysterious art of managing talented people is chief among them). Others are solved for one generation and then crop up years later in response to new market conditions. Still others really do get settled—at least for one set of people in one place. Our hope is that the pieces in this volume—the big themes they raise, the big ideas they put forward, and the practical guidance they detail—will help business leaders solve today's critical challenges in their own jobs and organizations.

—The Editors

HBR'S 10 MUST READS

The definitive
management ideas
of the year from
Harvard Business Review.

2015

Beware the Next Big Thing

by Julian Birkinshaw

WHERE DO NEW MANAGEMENT practices come from? A few emerge fully formed from the minds of academics and consultants, but the vast majority come from corporate executives experimenting with new ideas in their own organizations. A case in point is the online retailer Zappos, which is replacing its traditional hierarchy with a self-organizing "operating system" known as holacracy.

Zappos's experiment is getting a lot of attention. Like many management innovations before it, holacracy has an exciting zeitgeist appeal. At least a few executives in other firms are no doubt asking themselves, given today's pressure to innovate and the changing nature of the workforce, is this the management idea of the moment? Could it give my company a competitive edge? What are the risks of trying to import it?

For decades, executives have been asking similar questions whenever management innovations burst onto the scene. Sometimes a new idea is so transformative that it can and often does propel a company to unprecedented levels of performance. Six Sigma and lean manufacturing have had that effect, galvanizing managers to improve quality and cut costs.

But importing ideas is risky. Even the most obviously useful theory or practice can go wrong if a company is unprepared to act on the insights it offers. And the value of most management ideas—and where they might take you—is far from obvious. Is holacracy about empowering creativity or about tearing down authority? Can you envision "everyone" in your firm becoming a leader? Could your culture and organizational structure withstand such a dramatic change? The potential rewards of experimental concepts may be great for certain firms under certain circumstances, but for others, implementing them can be profoundly difficult or even destructive.

By taking deliberate steps to understand other companies' innovations and how they relate to your own firm's ways of thinking and functioning, you can better discern which experimental concepts are worth your while. With thoughtfulness and care, you can increase your chances of success when you do borrow ideas and, in the process, acquire new knowledge that will help improve your business in the long run.

It's the Next Big Thing! (Or Is It?)

Any radical management innovation is quick to attract the attention of journalists, academics, and consultants. My studies, which I conducted with Stefano Turconi, a research associate at London Business School, reveal important benefits of that attention: Researchers and writers help companies codify or make sense of their ideas, and the visibility helps executives build support for their practices inside and outside the firm. The public discussion lets other companies know about the idea.

Publicity also has a downside: It raises the risk of hype, disappointment, and, sometimes, a repudiation of the idea. (See the sidebar "The Inevitable Hype Cycle" later in this article.) This magazine, for example, has debuted ideas that are now part of the management canon—and ideas that have been relegated to the dusty archive shelves. Your goal as a manager couldn't be more different from those of the media and academia. You're not trying to ride the next wave; you're looking for the perfect wave. Popular opinion has less pertinence for you than an idea's underlying concepts; indeed, it's worth bearing in mind that foundational ideas often live on even after the practices associated with them have fallen from favor.

Idea in Brief

The Problem

Innovative management ideas that bubble up in other companies pose a perennial quandary: Should you attempt to borrow them, and if so, which ones and how? Even the most promising practices can fail if they're transplanted in the wrong firm.

The Solution

The best approach is to extract the essential principle from a management innovation—its underlying logic—by asking a series of questions about it, including: How is your company different from the originating firm? Are the innovation's goals worthwhile for your organization? Even if you decide the idea isn't right for you, the analysis can help you better understand your own management models and sharpen your practices.

So how can managers effectively look beyond hype to make sense of the ever-changing landscape of management innovation? Broadly speaking, there are two ways to borrow from innovative companies: observe-and-apply, and extract the central idea. Each offers benefits, and each has its own challenges.

Observe-and-apply

This is the most obvious—and most commonly employed—approach for adopting new management ideas. It can and does work well, but only under limited sets of circumstances. One is when the observed practice easily stands alone or involves just a small constellation of supporting behaviors. GE's well-regarded succession-planning process is a good example—think of the smooth CEO transition from Jack Welch to Jeffrey Immelt in 2000. The process is supported by just a few specific actions, including creating transparency around the candidates and planning for the likely departures of those who don't get the job. These behaviors are relatively easy to copy; thus it's common to see GE-inspired succession systems running well in other companies—for example, Walmart, GlaxoSmithKline, and Tesco.

Observe-and-apply also can work effectively when a company's management model or way of thinking is very similar to the originator's. Two software firms using the Agile development approach, for instance, are most likely employing many of the same techniques and a common language, so if one of them were to put a new management model into place, the other would be likely to replicate it successfully with observe-and-apply. Similarly, companies that have unorthodox ways of doing things are much more likely to succeed in borrowing management innovations from other nontraditional firms: Radical ideas tend to take hold when they move with, rather than against, the tide.

For that reason, I give Zappos a good chance of succeeding as it implements holacracy, an idea that originated in a couple of Silicon Valley start-ups. Zappos has already shown a proclivity to go its own way; the company is known for such unorthodox practices as testing employees' loyalty by offering them cash to quit.

But all too often, the practices used successfully at one company prove disastrous at another. Consider GE's high-performance culture in the late 1990s. Employees generally recognized that the firm's strong focus on individual accountability was first and foremost a means for honing corporate competitiveness in the marketplace. That understanding formed the backdrop for Welch's policy of ranking all employees within a given unit, rewarding and promoting the high performers, and firing (or providing remedial training for) the bottom 10%. The "rank and yank" system was emulated widely—but it often failed, particularly in organizations that hadn't developed cultures of productive internal competition. Employees unaccustomed to the pressure frequently responded in dysfunctional ways. At Microsoft, for example, rank and yank ended up pitting employees against one another and diverting their attention from competing against other companies.

More recently, a number of firms in the UK and Europe have sought to emulate some of the British retailer John Lewis's well-publicized management practices: generous benefits packages, inclusion of employee input in the selection of top executives, and a rewards scheme giving frontline workers the same annual bonus (as a percentage of salary) as the company's chief executive. These practices have helped the retailer attain an industry-leading position in employee engagement and retention. But the ideas haven't been easy for shareholder-owned companies to adopt. For one thing, John Lewis's practices are all of a piece—they fit well with and reinforce one another. A strong focus on training and development, for example, supports the firm's highly selective hiring process and its emphasis on internal promotion. For another, they grew organically out of an employee-centric philosophy that goes back to the company's founding as a worker-owned partnership. Removed from that context, egalitarian policies often fail to win support from executives and shareholders.

Google's policy of allowing employees to spend 20% of their time on innovation is another favorite target of the observe-and-apply approach (even though the company has now placed limits on the program to prevent developers from going off in too many directions at once). The policy is appealingly simple, and managers in other organizations are understandably attracted by its promise of churning out breakthrough ideas. But when other firms adopt the practice, the results are typically underwhelming. Managerial attitude is one reason. Google's top executives (initially, at least) were enthusiastic champions of the concept; in many companies, such management support is harder to come by. Also, Google is blessed with hotshot developers eager to pursue their brilliant ideas; developers who are unfamiliar with open-ended experimentation often find that they don't know what to do with their innovation time. For these reasons, companies that emulate the policy typically terminate it before the 20% projects have been given a chance to succeed.

It hardly needs pointing out that failure can cause a great deal of damage. Adopting and then abandoning new practices can wear out an organization and reduce the likelihood that leaders will be able to bring about sustained improvement. That's why companies need to use the observe-and-apply method with care.

Extract the central idea
The hazards of importing a management innovation can be greatly minimized by extracting only the essential principles of a practice. Whatever differences may exist between the new organizational

context and the original become less important, and fewer adjustments are required for the principles to take root.

UBS Wealth Management provides a good example. Following a successful merger in 2000, the financial services firm was seeking ways to grow. While brainstorming, the leadership team realized that one of the biggest obstacles to growth was the company's budgeting process—in particular, the time-consuming negotiations it required between headquarters and operating units. One executive suggested that the company could learn from the banking firm Svenska Handelsbanken, which had done away with budgeting a decade earlier. A group of senior managers visited the Swedish firm and saw that even though the companies' business models differed, it would be possible to borrow several of Handelsbanken's planning principles: less oversight from headquarters, greater frontline responsibility, and friendly competition among peer units. The team put together its own light-touch budgeting model, which was better suited to UBS's culture. For example, rather than adopt Handelsbanken's collective-bonus plan, which was based on groupwide performance, UBS linked bonuses to units' return-on-investment performance relative to that of peer groups.

Another example comes from GlaxoSmithKline. In the late 1990s, when the biotech revolution was threatening the pharmaceutical industry's R&D model, a few pharma firms, including Roche and Bristol-Myers Squibb, spent large sums buying biotech firms in order to gain access to their strong pipelines of innovative ideas. GSK tried something bolder: It studied the start-ups and determined that a key reason for their success was that they built cross-functional teams and focused them on specific therapeutic areas, a radical departure from pharma's traditions. GSK replicated the essence of that model internally, first creating semiautonomous Centres of Excellence for drug discovery and then breaking them down further into Discovery Performance Units, comprising 30 to 60 people, which were expected to seek funding for research projects from an internal investment board. While this model created some management challenges, it helped GSK retain its position as one of the world's

The Inevitable Hype Cycle

YOU CAN OFTEN GAIN valuable insight from radical management innovations, even if they fizzle out. And they do fizzle out. Nine-tenths of the approximately 100 branded management ideas I've studied lost their popularity within a decade or so. These include GE's Work-Out, W.L. Gore's lattice structure, Xerox's communities of practice, Thermo Electron's Spinout model, and Google's 20% innovation time policy.

Oticon's Spaghetti Organization is typical. In the early 1990s, soon after the Danish hearing-aid manufacturer began empowering employees to create their own development projects, the experiment was the subject of effusive praise. The company was inundated with queries from other businesses, and its executives hit the speaker circuit. But within a few years Oticon began to realize that its new-product portfolio lacked coherence and that too many resources were being wasted on projects that went nowhere.

Oticon's executives began shifting back toward a traditional structure, with project reviews becoming more formal and employees moving between tasks less frequently. Consultants began to cite the practice as a negative example, and in 2003 an academic analysis labeled the experiment a "partial failure."

Oticon's experience was more nuanced than the hype cycle suggests, however. Sales and profits increased during the early phases of the Spaghetti Organization, and when executives scaled back and used a modified form of the original practice, sales and profits continued to rise. Moreover, adopting the spaghetti structure served to shake things up—arguably an important step in the company's successful transformation, even though most of the practices introduced in the early 1990s have now disappeared.

To prevent the hype cycle from distracting you, look at how a management practice is really being used. Is it fulfilling its intended purpose in the company that originated it? That will help you ignore the talk of "breakthroughs" and "failures" and see what is simply useful about an idea.

top pharmaceutical companies and develop a drug pipeline that is among the industry's best.

Extracting the principle does not always work, of course, for a couple of reasons. First, identifying the underlying principle isn't a trivial matter. We are all prisoners of our own experience and cognitive biases. It's also often difficult to see the forest for the trees.

During the 1990s, for example, Ford tried everything it could think of—automation, training, quality circles—to match Toyota's high standards on cost and quality. But it didn't succeed in its effort, because it overlooked the essence of Toyota's system: a belief in employees' problem-solving skills.

A second, linked problem is that even when the underlying principle has been identified, it is often very difficult to put into use. When I was working with executives of a large investment bank to implement cross-functional collaboration, we easily identified the practice's enabling factors—common goals, transparent communication, and motivation to share knowledge—but implementation turned out to be impossible. The company's bonus culture, which focused on individual performance, was so deeply entrenched that it shaped everyone's behavior, and all attempts to encourage collaboration were doomed to fail.

Know Yourself Better

Regardless of the method you choose, corporate self-awareness is a powerful advantage. Not only can it help companies adopt the right innovations, but it can improve the planning and implementation of any major initiative. The organizational learning that results is an added benefit: An experiment, even if it's eventually deemed unsuccessful, serves as a stimulus for revisiting your existing management models in light of the imported ideas. That new knowledge can help your firm sharpen and improve its current practices.

Consider Roche, the Swiss pharma company. (Disclosure: I've done consulting work for Roche.) A team of its executives were intrigued by the practice, in use at other companies, of open innovation. They decided to experiment with InnoCentive, a web platform on which companies can present technical challenges to thousands of would-be solvers. The executives posted a thorny technical problem that the R&D team had been struggling with, and they got back imaginative and useful ideas. Encouraged, they tried a few more.

Four Kinds of Deviants

WHEN YOU'RE DECIDING whether to import a management innovation from another firm, it's crucial to consider the source. Most innovations originate in companies that might be called "deviants," in that they don't follow the crowd. But not all deviants are alike. Be careful which firms you borrow from.

- **Upstarts.** These are young, small, sometimes intentionally iconoclastic firms. Valve Corporation, a video game developer, expects employees to set their own hours, select their own projects, and migrate from team to team. In fact, employees are encouraged to move their desks to where the action is. Of course, it's easy to be unconventional when you're small. Don't expect an upstart's experiments to work in a larger, established company.

- **Related species.** These aren't business organizations, but they can provide useful insights. Alcoholics Anonymous, for instance, shows how an organization with a clear sense of purpose can function with no formal control systems. These organizations' management ideas are usually better admired from afar than implemented in a profit-making company, though their unusual principles can sometimes be a source of inspiration when handled with care.

- **Certified weird.** These are highly successful companies that, despite their large size, operate by their own rules. California-based tomato processor Morning Star has gotten along without managers for more than two decades. But virtually all such companies have governance models such as family ownership or trusts that help them maintain their individuality—Morning Star is privately held, for example. Beware of adopting their ideas unless your company has mechanisms for shielding it from day-to-day shareholder pressure.

- **Dancing giants.** These are big, traditional companies that have experimented with unusual models. Haier, the Chinese manufacturer, has created a highly decentralized budgeting process that pushes accountability down to individual teams. Shell's GameChanger, an innovative R&D funding model, has successfully nurtured many new technologies. Dancing giants' practices can be great sources of ideas, because they've already withstood shareholder scrutiny.

But after 10 challenges, they found that the implementation of the results by Roche's scientists and engineers was inconsistent. Solutions to process-related problems tended to be readily

9

implemented, but solutions to deeper scientific questions, for some reason, often were set aside and left unused. The experience helped the company see that there's no single best way to innovate; as a consequence, Roche moved toward establishing a portfolio of innovation approaches that could be matched with a range of challenges.

Or consider a software firm we studied that provides security services to clients in the financial, logistics, and public sectors. The founder had long been frustrated by the complexity and inflexibility of the project-planning methodologies commonly used in the software industry. Inspired by the auction-like models that recruitment consultancies use to find candidates, the founder came up with the idea of having employees bid to work on projects by touting their skills and interests.

The new model had benefits but also some flaws. Developers felt a loss of control: If they were passed over, they often didn't know why, and they had no way to further plead their cases. The firm decided to reduce the auction emphasis, shifting project-staffing decisions to a weekly meeting where everyone in the company was represented. Decisions took into account the needs not only of clients and project teams but also of individual developers. The company's new system still looks a lot like the traditional model used in many software companies, but it functions better, because of managers' new understanding of how to involve developers in the process.

Remember, when an experiment fails, resist the default response of shutting it down and pretending it never happened. Learning from failure is never glamorous or easy, but the lessons can be invaluable.

Moving Forward

Let's now look at the practical steps you should take in evaluating and importing management innovations.

Bide your time

The first thing to be done when another company's management experiment comes to your notice is nothing at all. It's wise to wait for a couple of years before you even consider borrowing an idea, either in whole or in part. Every new practice needs time to succeed or fail, and it's almost always a good idea to let the faddishness fade. Don't fall for the practice's charms too readily, but don't dismiss the idea entirely either, as the experimenting company might well be onto something.

Deconstruct the management model

Once you've decided to go ahead, you need to start by asking pointed questions to uncover the essence of the idea. During this stage, it's often useful to bring in outsiders who can offer a fresh perspective. Questions may include:

- *What is the underlying logic for this way of working?* For example, HCL Technologies' system for providing open 360-degree feedback to its managers is based on a simple logic of transparency.

- *What unusual assumptions is the originating company making about human behavior or the workings of the market?* Zappos's experiment with holacracy assumes that the benefits of self-organization outweigh its costs.

- *What inspiration or insights did the company draw on to come up with this model?* GSK's internal market model for drug development was inspired by the successful venture-capital-backed biotech model in California.

Understand the hypotheses

Ideally, you'll find that the originating company is testing a simple hypothesis or two, whether it is aware of doing so or not. For example, if the practice you're analyzing is the posting of managers' 360-degree feedback results, the working hypothesis might be that the policy will make managers more accountable to their employees. If you're experimenting with giving people greater freedom to work from home, the hypothesis might be that flexible working arrangements increase employees' level of engagement and, ultimately, their productivity.

Look for results

Next, analyze the originating company's results. Are the hypotheses supported, as social scientists would say? Does the posting of 360-degree feedback indeed result in greater accountability for managers? What are the practice's side effects? Talk to a few people at the company: Do you see evidence that managers are gaming the system? Keep digging deeper: Is more accountability to employees a good thing? If so, are there better, perhaps less disruptive, ways to achieve that end?

Make sure to look objectively at your own company. How is it similar to the originating firm? How is it different? Is your firm innovative or nontraditional enough for the new idea to take hold? Would your bureaucracy pose an insurmountable obstacle?

Experiment

If you see problems looming, be realistic. It's much easier to reconsider importing an idea before you've begun than to shut down an established initiative. But if you've done your due diligence and you're still excited about the idea, get to work creating an experiment of your own, with hypotheses, methods, and expected results: for example, "We hypothesize that by posting managers' 360-degree feedback online, we will see significant increases in employee satisfaction and retention rates within one year." Then you can begin collecting data to see whether the new practice is working and producing value for your firm.

It's easy to get so swept up in the glamour of a new idea that the prospect of implementing it seems straightforward. But remember that successful management innovators typically had to work very hard, over many years, to put their new ideas into place. Applying those ideas inside your own company is likely to take even longer.

My years of researching management ideas show that despite the challenges, the rewards of adoption can be great. Not only do you stand to make a real difference in your company, but there's also a wealth of knowledge to be gained from experiments. If your company analyzes the implementation carefully, it's bound to acquire skills as well as greater levels of awareness, and this new understanding can significantly improve your business.

Originally published in May 2014. Reprint R1405B

The Capitalist's Dilemma

by Clayton M. Christensen and Derek van Bever

LIKE AN OLD MACHINE emitting a new and troubling sound that even the best mechanics can't diagnose, the world economy continues its halting recovery from the 2008 recession. Look at what's happening in the United States: Even today, 60 months after the scorekeepers declared the recession to be over, its economy is still grinding along, producing low growth and disappointing job numbers.

One phenomenon we've observed is that, despite historically low interest rates, corporations are sitting on massive amounts of cash and failing to invest in innovations that might foster growth. That got us thinking: What is causing that behavior? Are great opportunities in short supply, or are executives failing to recognize them? And how is this behavior pattern linked to overall economic sluggishness? What is holding growth back?

Most theories of growth are developed at the macroeconomic level—at 30,000 feet. That perspective is good for spotting *correlations* between innovation and growth. To understand what *causes* growth, however, you have to crawl inside companies—and inside the minds of the people who invest in and manage them. This article (which builds on a *New York Times* piece Clay wrote in late 2012) is an attempt to form a theory from the ground up, by looking at company experience.

About a year ago we invited the students and alumni of our Harvard Business School course "Building and Sustaining a Successful Enterprise"—who represent a cross-section of the corporate, entrepreneurial, and financial services sectors worldwide—to join us in this effort. (See "A New Approach to Research.") Early on, we explored a wide range of reasons for the sputtering recovery, including political and economic uncertainty, the low rate of bank lending, a decline in publicly supported research in the United States, and the demise of innovation platforms like Bell Labs. (In "The Price of Wall Street's Power" our colleague Gautam Mukunda contends that the finance sector's growing power is a major factor.)

Fairly quickly, though, the discussion focused in on what had first attracted our attention: the choices companies make when they invest in innovation. Unlike some complicated macroeconomic factors, these choices are well within managers' control.

We're happy to report that we think we've figured out why managers are sitting on their hands, afraid to pursue what they see as risky innovations. We believe that such investments, viewed properly, would offer the surest path to profitable economic and job growth. In this article we advance some prescriptions that could become the basis of an agenda for meaningful progress in this area.

In our view the crux of the problem is that investments in different types of innovation affect economies (and companies) in very different ways—but are evaluated using the same (flawed) metrics. Specifically, financial markets—and companies themselves—use assessment metrics that make innovations that eliminate jobs more attractive than those that create jobs. We'll argue that the reliance on those metrics is based on the outdated assumption that capital is, in George Gilder's language, a "scarce resource" that should be conserved at all costs. But, as we will explain further, capital is no longer in short supply—witness the $1.6 trillion in cash on corporate balance sheets—and, if companies want to maximize returns on it, they must stop behaving as if it were. We would contend that the ability to attract talent, and the processes and resolve to deploy it against growth opportunities, are far harder to come by than cash. The tools

Idea in Brief

The Problem

What is the connection between slow growth in the U.S. economy and corporate reluctance to invest in market-creating innovations?

The Analysis

Investors and executives have been trained to think of capital as their scarcest resource—and this has led to unhelpful ways of assessing investment opportunities.

The Solution

We need new ways to measure potential and to define success.

businesses use to judge investments and their understanding of what is scarce and costly need to catch up with that new reality.

Before we get to the solutions, let's look more closely at the different types of innovation.

Three Kinds of Innovation

The seminal concepts of *disruptive* and *sustaining* innovations were developed by Clay as he was studying competition among companies. They relate to the process by which innovations become dominant in established markets and new entrants challenge incumbents. The focus of this article, however, is the *outcome* of innovations— their impact on growth. This shift requires us to categorize innovation in a slightly different way:

Performance-improving innovations replace old products with new and better models. They generally create few jobs because they're substitutive: When customers buy the new product, they usually don't buy the old product. When Toyota sells a Prius, the customer rarely buys a Camry too. Clay's book *The Innovator's Solution* characterized these as sustaining innovations, noting that the resource allocation processes of all successful incumbent firms are tuned to produce them repeatedly and consistently.

Efficiency innovations help companies make and sell mature, established products or services to the same customers at lower prices.

A New Approach to Research

IN WRITING THIS ARTICLE, we asked students and alumni of our HBS course "Building and Sustaining a Successful Enterprise" to collaborate with us. This collaboration took place primarily on the OpenIDEO online platform, which Tom Hulme, one of our alumni, helped develop, and was made possible through the leadership of the HBS Digital Initiative under the direction of Karim Lakhani. This effort represents a first attempt to create a community of lifelong collaboration with HBS alumni. Where we have been given permission, we share some of the individual contributions in this article.

Some of these innovations are what we have elsewhere called low-end disruptions, and they involve the creation of a new business model. Walmart was a low-end disrupter in retailing, for example, and Geico in insurance. Other innovations, such as Toyota's just-in-time production system, are process improvements. Efficiency innovations play two important roles. First, they raise productivity, which is essential for maintaining competitiveness but has the painful side effect of eliminating jobs. Second, they free up capital for more-productive uses. Toyota's production system, for example, allowed the automaker to operate with two months'—rather than two years'—worth of inventory on hand, which freed up massive amounts of cash.

Market-creating innovations, our third category, transform complicated or costly products so radically that they create a *new* class of consumers, or a new market. Look at what has happened with computers: The mainframe computer cost hundreds of thousands of dollars and was available to a very small group. Then the personal computer brought the price down to $2,000, which made it available to millions of people in the developed world. In turn, the smartphone made a $200 computer available to billions of people throughout the world. We see this pattern so frequently that we're tempted to offer it as an axiom: If only the skilled and the rich have access to a product or a service, then you can reasonably assume the existence of a market-creating opportunity.

Market-creating innovations have two critical ingredients. One is an enabling technology that drives down costs as volume grows. The other is a new business model allowing the innovator to reach

Jobless recoveries

In the recessions the United States has experienced since 1948, the rebound in employment has typically lagged the rebound in GDP by about six months. Since 1990, though, the lag has been increasing dramatically. But with the latest recession, 39 months after GDP had returned to normal, employment still hadn't caught up, and it was expected to lag for another two to three months.

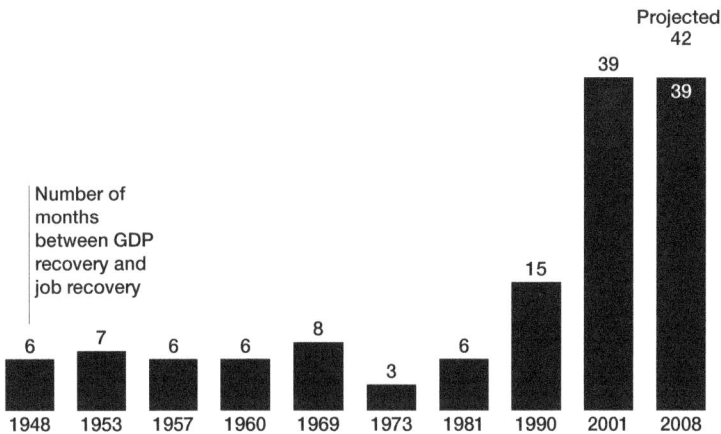

Projected
42

Number of
months
between GDP
recovery and
job recovery

1948	1953	1957	1960	1969	1973	1981	1990	2001	2008
6	7	6	6	8	3	6	15	39	39

Source: U.S. Bureau of Labor Statistics, U.S. Bureau of Economic Analysis, McKinsey Global Institute Analysis

people who have not been customers (often because they couldn't afford the original product). Think of it like this: An efficiency innovation pointed in the right direction—toward turning nonconsumption into consumption—becomes a market-creating innovation. Ford's Model T, for example, brought automobile ownership within reach for most Americans, because of both its simple design and the revolutionary assembly line that brought scale to the enterprise. In the same way, Texas Instruments and Hewlett-Packard used solid-state technology to bring low-cost calculators to millions of students and engineers worldwide.

Companies that develop market-creating innovations usually generate new jobs internally. When more people can buy their products, they need more employees to build, distribute, sell, and support them. A great deal of related employment growth, though, occurs in the innovating companies' supply chains or in partners whose own innovations help build a new platform. A classic example is the Bessemer Converter, patented in 1856, which made it possible to manufacture steel inexpensively for the first time. Andrew Carnegie used its revolutionary cost-reduction potential to build the Thomson Steel Works, but the railroad companies used the cheaper steel to create a new industry. U.S. steel employment quadrupled in the last quarter of the 19th century, reaching 180,000 by 1900, and railroad employment reached 1.8 million a scant two decades later.

The combination of a technology that drives down costs with the ambition to eradicate nonconsumption—to serve new customers who want to get something done—can have a revolutionary effect. A decade ago, Apple's managers were on the lookout for a device that could enable convenient, affordable storage of a consumer's music library, with anytime, anywhere access. They saw in Toshiba's development of a 1.8-inch hard drive the opportunity to fulfill this job, which triggered the development of the iPod/iTunes business model. And if companies such as Corning and Global Crossing hadn't innovated to create and lay ample low-cost dark fiber capacity, Google, Amazon, and Facebook wouldn't exist as we know them today.

Market-creating innovations need capital to grow—sometimes a *lot* of capital. But they also create a *lot* of jobs, even though job generation is not an intended effect but a happy consequence. Efficiency innovations are at work 24/7 in every industry; that very same efficiency, if targeted toward making a product or a service more affordable and accessible, can create net new jobs, not eliminate them.

The mix of these types of innovation—performance-improving, efficiency, and market-creating—has a major impact on the job growth of nations, industries, and companies. The dials on the three types of innovation are sensitive, but if the capital that efficiency innovations liberate is invested in market-creating innovations at scale, the economy works quite well. However, that's a big "if," as we shall see.

The Orthodoxy of New Finance

So, to come back to our central question (phrased in a new way): Why do companies invest primarily in efficiency innovations, which eliminate jobs, rather than market-creating innovations, which generate them? A big part of the answer lies in an unexamined economic assumption. The assumption—which has risen almost to the level of a religion—is that corporate performance should be focused on, and measured by, how efficiently capital is used. This belief has an extraordinary impact on how both investors and managers assess opportunities. And it's at the root of what we call the *capitalist's dilemma.*

Let's back up to see where this assumption came from. A fundamental tenet of economics is that some of the inputs required to make a product or service are abundant and cheap—like sand. We don't need to account for such inputs and can waste them, if need be. Others are scarce and costly and must be husbanded carefully. Historically, capital was scarce and costly. So investors and managers alike were taught to maximize the revenue and profit per dollar of capital deployed.

While it's still true that scarce resources need to be managed closely, it's no longer true that capital is scarce. A recent Bain & Company analysis captures this point nicely, concluding that we have entered a new environment of "capital superabundance." Bain estimates that total financial assets are today almost 10 times the value of the global output of all goods and services, and that the development of financial sectors in emerging economies will cause global capital to grow another 50% by 2020. We are awash in capital.

Because they were taught to believe that the *efficiency* of capital was a virtue, financiers began measuring profitability not as dollars, yen, or yuan, but as *ratios* like RONA (return on net assets), ROIC (return on invested capital), and IRR (internal rate of return).

Do We Need a Revolution?

THE ORTHODOXIES GOVERNING FINANCE are so entrenched that we almost need a modern-day Martin Luther to articulate the need for change. Here's what reform might address:

Thesis 1. **We need new ways to assess investments in innovation.** Our success metrics determine what we can and cannot invest in. We have allowed a minority to dictate those metrics to the majority. Over and over, the higher value placed on return on net assets, internal rate of return, and earnings per share over other metrics has led to innovations that squeeze costs and noncash assets. As a result, investing to create growth and jobs is a third-best option, behind efficiency innovations (first) and doing nothing (second).

Thesis 2. **We should no longer husband capital. It is abundant and cheap. We should use it, not hoard it.** What managers see inside their company's resource allocation processes likely does not reflect the new reality in the economy and in the capital markets. Hurdle rates aren't handed down by a deity; they can (and should) be changed as the cost of capital changes.

Thesis 3. **We need new tools for managing the resources that *are* scarce and costly.** How would we measure the success of investments in making good people better, for example, or in our ability to attract and retain talent? What if we prioritized time as a scarce resource?

These ratios are simply fractions, comprising a numerator and a denominator, but they gave investors and managers twice the number of levers to pull to improve their measured performance. To drive RONA or ROIC up, they could generate more profit to add to the numerator, of course. But if that seemed daunting, they could focus on reducing the denominator—outsourcing more, wiping more assets off the balance sheet. Either way, the ratio would improve. Similarly, they could increase IRR either by generating more profit to grow the numerator or by reducing the denominator—which is essentially the time required to get the return. If they invested only in projects that paid off quickly, then IRR would go up.

All of this makes market-creating innovations appear less attractive as investments. Typically, they bear fruit only after five to 10 years; in contrast, efficiency innovations typically pay off within a year or two. What's worse, growing market-creating innovations to scale uses capital, which must often be put onto the balance sheet. Efficiency innovations take capital off the balance sheet, however. To top it off, efficiency innovations almost always seem to entail less risk than market-creating ones, because a market for them already exists. Any way you look at it, if you measure investments using these ratios, efficiency innovations always appear to be a better deal.

What Has Become of the Long-Term Investor?

One might expect that, even if this approach to measurement appealed to short-term investors, we'd see countervailing pressure from institutional investors, who are ostensibly focused on long-term value creation. Take pension funds, the largest category of investor globally, representing more than $30 trillion in assets, almost $20 trillion of that just in U.S. pension funds. In theory, no investor is better positioned to model "patient capital" behavior. However, for the most part pension funds don't demonstrate patience: In fact, they have led the pack in the search for high short-term returns. One of the most spirited exchanges among our alumni centered on that apparently self-defeating behavior and what, if anything, might be done about it. It turns out that because of a variety of factors—depressed returns, substantial unfunded commitments, and longer life expectancies—the funds aren't growing fast enough to meet their obligations. So they look for quick payoffs and demand that the companies they invest in, and the managers they invest with, meet high hurdle rates. A failure to adjust expectations—and hurdle rates—will keep pension funds on the sidelines in coming years, making a bad situation even worse.

Venture capitalists might also be expected to look past ratio-centric metrics, since market creation appears to be their focus. And many VCs do. But many others invest mostly in companies that are developing performance-improving and efficiency innovations and can be sold within a couple of years to a large industry incumbent. Several of our alumni noted this bias in their interactions with VCs, many of whom are drawn to business plans that target well-defined markets, just as corporate executives are.

What about the low cost of capital? Shouldn't that create incentives for corporate managers—and outside investors—to invest their cash in ambitious market-creating innovations? Technically, it is true that the cost of capital is low—indeed, the Fed's interest rate for lending to banks is near zero. But neither companies nor investors experience it like that. Entrepreneurs claim in their business plans that investors will make their money back five times over. Venture capitalists ask for even higher returns. Internal corporate business plans routinely promise returns from 20% to 25%—because that is the historical corporate cost of equity capital. Investors and managers were all taught that calculations of the present value of potential investments should be based on that corporate cost, adjusted for differences in risk. From the perspective of the individuals seeking funding, the *quoted list price* of capital before making the investment is anything but zero.

What individuals don't observe, however, is that the actual return investors of the capital receive after it has been deployed is, on average, approaching zero. Today every attractive opportunity is being eyed by many more investors—and also being pursued by many more companies—than was the case in the past. All the competition drives the price of the deals so high that the returns to investors are dramatically compromised. For nearly a decade, the actual returns of all VC-backed investments, which were promised to be at least 25%, have totaled up to zero every year. Professor William Sahlman named this paradox "capital market myopia."

Year after year, public U.S. corporations announce plans to invest in new growth markets. And yet if you dig into their research and development budgets, you'll find that very little of that money targets market-creating innovations. Some is being spent on performance-improving innovations, but the lion's share is allocated to efficiency innovations. And more than the executives of these enterprises imagine. One of our alumni noted the recent ascendance of the metric "return on research capital" (RORC). This measure, current year profit over prior year research expenditure, justifies only the most tightly scoped performance-improving or efficiency innovations.

Our alumni expressed deep frustration over the way that the resource allocation process is biased against profitable, high-growth opportunities in new markets and favors predictable investments focused on current customers. This leads to a paradox: Competing for a point of share in an established market appears to be easy, even in the face of fierce competition. Investing to create a new market appears to be hard, even in the absence of headwinds and with the prospect of a much more sizable, and profitable, opportunity. One recent alumnus, a product manager at a highly respected *Fortune* 100 manufacturer, noted, "We've lost the concept of having a portfolio of businesses. Out of every business we expect incremental improvement on these key financial metrics." He thought this produced a crowded, efficiency-focused, near-term agenda. "If I try to advocate for a different approach, the response will be, 'Sounds like an interesting idea—let's talk about it at the end of the fiscal year,'" he told us.

The result of all these interrelated failures is that the institutions meant to lubricate capitalism no longer do so. Banks, in particular, seem beset by boredom, unenthusiastic about actually making commercial loans, as many small and medium-size businesses will attest. This reluctance to lend is likely to erode banks' franchise permanently, as scores of alternative lending entities are being created to fill the void. The Federal Reserve, whose primary tool for stimulating the economy is increasing the supply of money and keeping interest rates low, doesn't work because interest is no longer a significant factor in businesses' cost structure.

This, then, is the capitalist's dilemma: Doing the right thing for long-term prosperity is the wrong thing for most investors, according to the tools used to guide investments. In our attempts to maximize returns to capital, we reduce returns to capital. Capitalists seem uninterested in capitalism—in supporting the development of market-creating innovations. Left unaddressed, the capitalist's dilemma might usher in an era of "post-capitalism." Adam Smith's "invisible hand" is meant to work behind the scenes, efficiently allocating capital and labor to sectors in which prices and returns are rising, and taking resources away from those in which they're falling. But if the cost of capital is insignificant, it emits only the faintest of signals to the invisible hand about where and when capital should flow.

Renewing the System

Although the reasons for the collective reluctance to invest in market-creating innovations are straightforward, they defy simple answers. Nonetheless, in the following paragraphs we'll propose four solutions worth exploring.

Repurposing capital

In contrast to the providers of capital, capital itself is highly malleable, in that certain policies can "convince" capital that it "wants" to do things differently. Today much of capital is what we might call *migratory*. It lacks a home. When invested, migratory capital wants to exit as quickly as possible and to take out as much additional capital as possible before it does. A second type of capital is *timid*. It is risk-averse. Much of timid capital resides as cash and equivalents on companies' balance sheets, where making no investment is better than making an investment that might fail. Another type is *enterprise* capital. Once injected into a company, enterprise capital likes to stay there. Resolving the capitalist's dilemma entails "persuading" migratory and timid capital to become enterprise capital.

One way to repurpose capital is through tax policy. Our alumni had a spirited exchange on the wisdom of imposing a Tobin tax on financial transactions to reduce high-frequency trading, which would increase illiquidity and therefore (it is thought) investment in innovation. Such a tax would be anything but simple to devise and enforce, but a growing body of academic and empirical evidence suggests it could be effective at repurposing capital by lengthening shareholder tenure.

A company-level approach would be to reward shareholders for loyalty. Our alumni suggested several ways to accomplish this. One is to align shareholder influence with shareholding period, allowing

When the World Is Awash in Capital

INTEL IS THE ONLY significant U.S. semiconductor company that still makes its own chips. If you measure profitability using return on assets, the other companies are much more profitable, for a simple reason: Outsourcing fabrication to contractors like Taiwan Semiconductor Manufacturing Company (TSMC) reduces the denominator in that ratio.

In 2009 Clay Christensen interviewed Morris Chang, founder of TSMC, about this phenomenon. Chang had been second-in-command at one of the most powerful semiconductor companies in America, Texas Instruments, before he returned to his native Taiwan and founded TSMC. At the time of this interview, TSMC was making more than half of all semiconductor circuits in the world.

Clay said to Chang, "Every time a new customer outsources to you, he peels assets off of his balance sheet, and in one way or another puts those assets on your balance sheet. You both can't be making the right decision."

"Yes, if you measure different things, both can be right," Chang replied. "The Americans like ratios, like RONA, EVA, ROCE, and so on. Driving assets off the balance sheets drives the ratios up. I keep looking. But so far I have not found a single bank that accepts deposits denominated in ratios. Banks only take currency.

"There is capital everywhere," Chang continued. "And it is cheap. So why are the Americans so afraid of using capital?"

voting power to vest over time the way employee stock options do. The alumnus who suggested this gave the following rationale: Why should investors who are mere tourists, holding stock for weeks or months, be given the same full voting power as long-term owners? Another method involves extra-share or extra-dividend mechanisms known as L-shares. The most popular L-share scheme in current use is a call warrant that's exercisable at a fixed time horizon and price if the share is held for the entire loyalty period.

These and other proposals to create loyalty shares and bonuses, and royalty shares that facilitate investment in targeted, long-term market development projects, are still a novelty and are subject to all manner of gaming, but they are coming up more often in board conversations and in corporate prospectuses.

Rebalancing business schools

Much as it pains us to say it, a lot of the blame for the capitalist's dilemma rests with our great schools of business, including our own. In mapping the terrain of business and management, we have routinely separated disciplines that can only properly be understood in terms of their interactions with one another, and we've advanced success metrics that are at best superficial and at worst harmful.

Finance is taught independently in most business schools. Strategy is taught independently, too—as if strategy could be conceived and implemented without finance. The reality is that finance will eat strategy for breakfast any day—financial logic will overwhelm strategic imperatives—unless we can develop approaches and models that allow each discipline to bring its best attributes to cooperative investment decision making. As long as we continue this siloed approach to the MBA curriculum and experience, our leading business schools run the risk of falling farther and farther behind the needs of sectors our graduates aspire to lead.

The intricate workings of the resource allocation process often are not studied at all in business schools. As a result, MBAs graduate with little sense of how decisions in one part of the enterprise relate to or reflect priorities in other parts. One of our alumni noted, "The only way we learned what projects to invest in was in FIN I [the introductory finance course at HBS]." A whole host of questions goes unasked—and unanswered: How do I identify conditions that signal opportunity for long-term, growth-creating investment? What proxies for estimated future cash flows can I use in evaluating an investment that is pointed toward a new market? How do we identify and build innovations that will help noncustomers perform jobs they need to get done? When are the traditional metrics of IRR and NPV most appropriate, and when are they likely to lead us astray? Since the functions of the enterprise are interdependent, we should mirror this in our teaching.

Realigning strategy and resource allocation

The alumni debated a number of potential solutions to the resource allocation processes' bias against market-creating opportunities. The solutions all were founded on the insight that setting the risk-adjusted cost of capital in the valuation of opportunities is a choice. If we are realistic about the true cost of capital, investing in the long term becomes easier.

The alumni also expressed broad support for bringing transparency to R&D spending through the creation of an "innovation scorecard" that categorized spending by the taxonomy we're developing here. The intent was to give leaders an internal tool for analyzing the innovation pipeline and the prospects for growth it contains.

Emancipating management

Many managers yearn to focus on the long term but don't think it's an option. Because investors' median holding period for shares is now about 10 months, executives feel pressure to maximize short-term returns. Many worry that if they don't meet the numbers, they will be replaced by someone who will. The job of a manager is thus reduced to sourcing, assembling, and shipping the numbers that deliver short-term gains.

While it's true that most companies, private and public, have shareholders who invest with an eye to the short term, they also have those who are focused on the long term—citizens, not tourists, to use the metaphor introduced earlier. The expectations of the two types of investors have diverged. Efforts to satisfy one group will conflict with the demands of the other. Because no policy can maximize returns for all shareholders, the only viable approach is to manage the company to maximize the value of the enterprise in the long run. It's the job of managers and academics alike to develop the tools to support this endeavor. They can make a good start by treating spreadsheets as a useful tool that complements strategic decision making but is not a substitute for it. (See "Spreadsheets: The Fast Food of Strategic Decision Making.")

The problem, of course, is not with our tools but with ourselves. As one alumnus noted in a very funny post, our ratios and tools tell us exactly what they claim to tell us: Return on assets is . . . the return on assets; DCF is . . . the discounted cash flows. The problem is in how the ratios are understood and applied. We have regressed

Spreadsheets: The Fast Food of Strategic Decision Making

JUST AS abundant, cheap fast food helped create an epidemic in obesity and diabetes, the popularity of spreadsheets has given rise to an unhealthy dependence on metrics like return on invested capital and internal rate of return.

Before 1978, when the spreadsheet was invented by a student at Harvard Business School, such metrics existed, but calculating them was cumbersome, since pro forma financials were done by hand with simple four-function calculators. These metrics were judiciously used as inputs, but investment decisions were rarely based on them.

The spreadsheet made it simple for analysts to build financial models of companies, allowing them to study how different inputs and assumptions affected the metrics of value. Armed with this tool, a 26-year-old Wall Street analyst could then sit across the desk from a CEO and tell her how to run her company. Not only that, the analyst could explain that "the market" would punish the CEO if she did not follow the orthodoxies of new finance, too. The rules of this game, by the way, were devised by the analysts themselves, tilting the playing field against the CEO and in favor of the analysts' spreadsheets—which were preprogrammed to predict when the CEO wouldn't meet an anticipated number and to set up a short sale or custom-made derivative.

Scott Cook, the founder and executive chairman of Intuit (an HBS alumnus who knows our course well), shared his views on what he sees as the tyranny of financial metrics. He has observed that a focus on financial outcomes too early in the innovation process produces "a withering of ambition." He argues that financial metrics lack predictive power. "Every one of our tragic and costly new business failures had a succession of great-looking financial spreadsheets," he says. Now new-product teams at Intuit do not submit a financial spreadsheet to begin work and testing; rather, he notes, they focus on "where we can change lives most profoundly."

In a very real sense, too many executives have outsourced the job of managerial judgment and decision making to this convenient—but ultimately unnutritious—tool. One simple way to put it in its proper place is to resolve never to begin or end an investment conversation with reference to a spreadsheet.

from the decades when Drucker and Levitt urged us not to define the boundaries of our businesses by products or SIC codes but to remember that the point of a business is to create a customer.

Dilemmas and paradoxes stymie capable people when they don't understand what surrounds them and why. That's the reason the innovator's dilemma historically has paralyzed so many smart managers. Managers who take the time to understand the innovator's dilemma, however, have been able to respond effectively when faced with disruption. Now it appears that we face a capitalist's dilemma. We hope that this attempt to frame the problem will inspire many of you to work with us to devise solutions to this dilemma, not just for the individual good that might result but for the long-term prosperity of us all.

Originally published in June 2014. Reprint R1406C

The Focused Leader

by Daniel Goleman

A PRIMARY TASK of leadership is to direct attention. To do so, leaders must learn to focus their own attention. When we speak about being focused, we commonly mean thinking about one thing while filtering out distractions. But a wealth of recent research in neuroscience shows that we focus in many ways, for different purposes, drawing on different neural pathways—some of which work in concert, while others tend to stand in opposition.

Grouping these modes of attention into three broad buckets—focusing on *yourself,* focusing on *others,* and focusing on *the wider world*—sheds new light on the practice of many essential leadership skills. Focusing inward and focusing constructively on others helps leaders cultivate the primary elements of emotional intelligence. A fuller understanding of how they focus on the wider world can improve their ability to devise strategy, innovate, and manage organizations.

Every leader needs to cultivate this triad of awareness, in abundance and in the proper balance, because a failure to focus inward leaves you rudderless, a failure to focus on others renders you clueless, and a failure to focus outward may leave you blindsided.

Focusing on Yourself

Emotional intelligence begins with self-awareness—getting in touch with your inner voice. Leaders who heed their inner voices can draw on more resources to make better decisions and connect with their authentic selves. But what does that entail? A look at how people focus inward can make this abstract concept more concrete.

Self-awareness

Hearing your inner voice is a matter of paying careful attention to internal physiological signals. These subtle cues are monitored by the insula, which is tucked behind the frontal lobes of the brain. Attention given to any part of the body amps up the insula's sensitivity to that part. Tune in to your heartbeat, and the insula activates more neurons in that circuitry. How well people can sense their heartbeats has, in fact, become a standard way to measure their self-awareness.

Gut feelings are messages from the insula and the amygdala, which the neuroscientist Antonio Damasio, of the University of Southern California, calls *somatic markers*. Those messages are sensations that something "feels" right or wrong. Somatic markers simplify decision making by guiding our attention toward better options. They're hardly foolproof (how often was that feeling that you left the stove on correct?), so the more comprehensively we read them, the better we use our intuition. (See "Are You Skimming This Sidebar?")

Consider, for example, the implications of an analysis of interviews conducted by a group of British researchers with 118 professional traders and 10 senior managers at four City of London investment banks. The most successful traders (whose annual income averaged £500,000) were neither the ones who relied entirely on analytics nor the ones who just went with their guts. They focused on a full range of emotions, which they used to judge the value of their intuition. When they suffered losses, they acknowledged their anxiety, became more cautious, and took fewer risks. The least successful traders (whose income averaged only £100,000) tended to ignore their anxiety and keep going with their guts. Because they failed to heed a wider array of internal signals, they were misled.

Zeroing in on sensory impressions of ourselves in the moment is one major element of self-awareness. But another is critical to lead-

Idea in Brief

The Problem

A primary task of leadership is to direct attention. To do so, leaders must learn to focus their own attention.

The Argument

People commonly think of "being focused" as filtering out distractions while concentrating on one thing. But a wealth of recent neuroscience research shows that we focus attention in many ways, for different purposes, while drawing on different neural pathways.

The Solution

Every leader needs to cultivate a triad of awareness—an inward focus, a focus on others, and an outward focus. Focusing inward and focusing on others helps leaders cultivate emotional intelligence. Focusing outward can improve their ability to devise strategy, innovate, and manage organizations.

ership: combining our experiences across time into a coherent view of our authentic selves.

To be authentic is to be the same person to others as you are to yourself. In part that entails paying attention to what others think of you, particularly people whose opinions you esteem and who will be candid in their feedback. A variety of focus that is useful here is *open awareness,* in which we broadly notice what's going on around us without getting caught up in or swept away by any particular thing. In this mode we don't judge, censor, or tune out; we simply perceive.

Leaders who are more accustomed to giving input than to receiving it may find this tricky. Someone who has trouble sustaining open awareness typically gets snagged by irritating details, such as fellow travelers in the airport security line who take forever getting their carry-ons into the scanner. Someone who can keep her attention in open mode will notice the travelers but not worry about them, and will take in more of her surroundings. (See the sidebar "Expand Your Awareness.")

Of course, being open to input doesn't guarantee that someone will provide it. Sadly, life affords us few chances to learn how others

Are You Skimming This Sidebar?

DO YOU HAVE TROUBLE remembering what someone has just told you in conversation? Did you drive to work this morning on autopilot? Do you focus more on your smartphone than on the person you're having lunch with?

Attention is a mental muscle; like any other muscle, it can be strengthened through the right kind of exercise. The fundamental rep for building deliberate attention is simple: When your mind wanders, notice that it has wandered, bring it back to your desired point of focus, and keep it there as long as you can. That basic exercise is at the root of virtually every kind of meditation. Meditation builds concentration and calmness and facilitates recovery from the agitation of stress.

So does a video game called Tenacity, now in development by a design group and neuroscientists at the University of Wisconsin. Slated for release in 2014, the game offers a leisurely journey through any of half a dozen scenes, from a barren desert to a fantasy staircase spiraling heavenward. At the beginner's level you tap an iPad screen with one finger every time you exhale; the challenge is to tap two fingers with every fifth breath. As you move to higher levels, you're presented with more distractions—a helicopter flies into view, a plane does a flip, a flock of birds suddenly scud by.

When players are attuned to the rhythm of their breathing, they experience the strengthening of selective attention as a feeling of calm focus, as in meditation. Stanford University is exploring that connection at its Calming Technology Lab, which is developing relaxing devices, such as a belt that detects your breathing rate. Should a chock-full in-box, for instance, trigger what has been called e-mail apnea, an iPhone app can guide you through exercises to calm your breathing and your mind.

really see us, and even fewer for executives as they rise through the ranks. That may be why one of the most popular and overenrolled courses at Harvard Business School is Bill George's Authentic Leadership Development, in which George has created what he calls True North groups to heighten this aspect of self-awareness.

These groups (which anyone can form) are based on the precept that self-knowledge begins with self-revelation. Accordingly, they are open and intimate, "a safe place," George explains, "where members can discuss personal issues they do not feel they can raise elsewhere—often not even with their closest family members."

Expand Your Awareness

JUST AS A CAMERA LENS can be set narrowly on a single point or more widely to take in a panoramic view, you can focus tightly or expansively.

One measure of open awareness presents people with a stream of letters and numbers, such as S, K, O, E, 4, R, T, 2, H, P. In scanning the stream, many people will notice the first number, 4, but after that their attention blinks. Those firmly in open awareness mode will register the second number as well.

Strengthening the ability to maintain open awareness requires leaders to do something that verges on the unnatural: cultivate at least sometimes a willingness to not be in control, not offer up their own views, not judge others. That's less a matter of deliberate action than of attitude adjustment.

One path to making that adjustment is through the classic power of positive thinking, because pessimism narrows our focus, whereas positive emotions widen our attention and our receptiveness to the new and unexpected. A simple way to shift into positive mode is to ask yourself, "If everything worked out perfectly in my life, what would I be doing in 10 years?" Why is that effective? Because when you're in an upbeat mood, the University of Wisconsin neuroscientist Richard Davidson has found, your brain's left prefrontal area lights up. That area harbors the circuitry that reminds us how great we'll feel when we reach some long-sought goal.

"Talking about positive goals and dreams activates brain centers that open you up to new possibilities," says Richard Boyatzis, a psychologist at Case Western Reserve. "But if you change the conversation to what you should do to fix yourself, it closes you down . . . . You need the negative to survive, but the positive to thrive."

What good does that do? "We don't know who we are until we hear ourselves speaking the story of our lives to those we trust," George says. It's a structured way to match our view of our true selves with the views our most trusted colleagues have—an external check on our authenticity.

Self-control

"Cognitive control" is the scientific term for putting one's attention where one wants it and keeping it there in the face of temptation to wander. This focus is one aspect of the brain's executive function, which is located in the prefrontal cortex. A colloquial term for it is "willpower."

Cognitive control enables executives to pursue a goal despite distractions and setbacks. The same neural circuitry that allows such a single-minded pursuit of goals also manages unruly emotions. Good cognitive control can be seen in people who stay calm in a crisis, tame their own agitation, and recover from a debacle or defeat.

Decades' worth of research demonstrates the singular importance of willpower to leadership success. Particularly compelling is a longitudinal study tracking the fates of all 1,037 children born during a single year in the 1970s in the New Zealand city of Dunedin. For several years during childhood the children were given a battery of tests of willpower, including the psychologist Walter Mischel's legendary "marshmallow test"—a choice between eating one marshmallow right away and getting two by waiting 15 minutes. In Mischel's experiments, roughly a third of children grab the marshmallow on the spot, another third hold out for a while longer, and a third manage to make it through the entire quarter hour.

Years later, when the children in the Dunedin study were in their 30s and all but 4% of them had been tracked down again, the researchers found that those who'd had the cognitive control to resist the marshmallow longest were significantly healthier, more successful financially, and more law-abiding than the ones who'd been unable to hold out at all. In fact, statistical analysis showed that a child's level of self-control was a more powerful predictor of financial success than IQ, social class, or family circumstance.

How we focus holds the key to exercising willpower, Mischel says. Three subvarieties of cognitive control are at play when you pit self-restraint against self-gratification: the ability to voluntarily disengage your focus from an object of desire; the ability to resist distraction so that you don't gravitate back to that object; and the ability to concentrate on the future goal and imagine how good you will feel when you achieve it. As adults the children of Dunedin may have been held hostage to their younger selves, but they need not have been, because the power to focus can be developed. (See the sidebar "Learning Self-Restraint.")

Learning Self-Restraint

QUICK, NOW. Here's a test of cognitive control. In what direction is the middle arrow in each row pointing?

$$\rightarrow \rightarrow \rightarrow \leftarrow \leftarrow$$

$$\rightarrow \leftarrow \leftarrow \leftarrow \leftarrow$$

$$\rightarrow \rightarrow \leftarrow \rightarrow \rightarrow$$

The test, called the Eriksen Flanker Task, gauges your susceptibility to distraction. When it's taken under laboratory conditions, differences of a thousandth of a second can be detected in the speed with which subjects perceive which direction the middle arrows are pointing. The stronger their cognitive control, the less susceptible they are to distraction.

Interventions to strengthen cognitive control can be as unsophisticated as a game of Simon Says or Red Light—any exercise in which you are asked to stop on cue. Research suggests that the better a child gets at playing Musical Chairs, the stronger his or her prefrontal wiring for cognitive control will become.

Operating on a similarly simple principle is a social and emotional learning (SEL) method that's used to strengthen cognitive control in schoolchildren across the United States. When confronted by an upsetting problem, the children are told to think of a traffic signal. The red light means stop, calm down, and think before you act. The yellow light means slow down and think of several possible solutions. The green light means try out a plan and see how it works. Thinking in these terms allows the children to shift away from amygdala-driven impulses to prefrontal-driven deliberate behavior.

It's never too late for adults to strengthen these circuits as well. Daily sessions of mindfulness practice work in a way similar to Musical Chairs and SEL. In these sessions you focus your attention on your breathing and practice tracking your thoughts and feelings without getting swept away by them. Whenever you notice that your mind has wandered, you simply return it to your breath. It sounds easy—but try it for 10 minutes, and you'll find there's a learning curve.

Focusing on Others

The word "attention" comes from the Latin *attendere,* meaning "to reach toward." This is a perfect definition of focus on others, which is the foundation of empathy and of an ability to build social relationships—the second and third pillars of emotional intelligence.

Executives who can effectively focus on others are easy to recognize. They are the ones who find common ground, whose opinions carry the most weight, and with whom other people want to work. They emerge as natural leaders regardless of organizational or social rank.

The empathy triad

We talk about empathy most commonly as a single attribute. But a close look at where leaders are focusing when they exhibit it reveals three distinct kinds, each important for leadership effectiveness:

- *cognitive empathy*—the ability to understand another person's perspective;

- *emotional empathy*—the ability to feel what someone else feels;

- *empathic concern*—the ability to sense what another person needs from you.

Cognitive empathy enables leaders to explain themselves in meaningful ways—a skill essential to getting the best performance from their direct reports. Contrary to what you might expect, exercising cognitive empathy requires leaders to think about feelings rather than to feel them directly.

An inquisitive nature feeds cognitive empathy. As one successful executive with this trait puts it, "I've always just wanted to learn everything, to understand anybody that I was around—why they thought what they did, why they did what they did, what worked for them, and what didn't work." But cognitive empathy is also an outgrowth of self-awareness. The executive circuits that allow us to think about our own thoughts and to monitor the feelings that flow from them let us apply the same reasoning to other people's minds when we choose to direct our attention that way.

Emotional empathy is important for effective mentoring, managing clients, and reading group dynamics. It springs from ancient parts of the brain beneath the cortex—the amygdala, the hypothalamus, the hippocampus, and the orbitofrontal cortex—that allow us to feel fast without thinking deeply. They tune us in by arousing in our bodies the emotional states of others: I literally feel your pain. My brain patterns match up with yours when I listen to you tell a gripping story. As Tania Singer, the director of the social neuroscience department at the Max Planck Institute for Human Cognitive and Brain Sciences, in Leipzig, says, "You need to understand your own feelings to understand the feelings of others." Accessing your capacity for emotional empathy depends on combining two kinds of attention: a deliberate focus on your own echoes of someone else's feelings and an open awareness of that person's face, voice, and other external signs of emotion. (See the sidebar "When Empathy Needs to Be Learned.")

Empathic concern, which is closely related to emotional empathy, enables you to sense not just how people feel but what they need from you. It's what you want in your doctor, your spouse—and your boss. Empathic concern has its roots in the circuitry that compels parents' attention to their children. Watch where people's eyes go when someone brings an adorable baby into a room, and you'll see this mammalian brain center leaping into action.

One neural theory holds that the response is triggered in the amygdala by the brain's radar for sensing danger and in the prefrontal cortex by the release of oxytocin, the chemical for caring. This implies that empathic concern is a double-edged feeling. We intuitively experience the distress of another as our own. But in deciding whether we will meet that person's needs, we deliberately weigh how much we value his or her well-being.

Getting this intuition-deliberation mix right has great implications. Those whose sympathetic feelings become too strong may themselves suffer. In the helping professions, this can lead to compassion fatigue; in executives, it can create distracting feelings of anxiety about people and circumstances that are beyond anyone's control. But those who protect themselves by deadening their feelings may lose touch with empathy. Empathic concern requires us to manage our personal distress without numbing ourselves to the pain of others. (See the sidebar "When Empathy Needs to Be Controlled.")

When Empathy Needs to Be Learned

EMOTIONAL EMPATHY can be developed. That's the conclusion suggested by research conducted with physicians by Helen Riess, the director of the Empathy and Relational Science Program at Boston's Massachusetts General Hospital. To help the physicians monitor themselves, she set up a program in which they learned to focus using deep, diaphragmatic breathing and to cultivate a certain detachment—to watch an interaction from the ceiling, as it were, rather than being lost in their own thoughts and feelings. "Suspending your own involvement to observe what's going on gives you a mindful awareness of the interaction without being completely reactive," says Riess. "You can see if your own physiology is charged up or balanced. You can notice what's transpiring in the situation." If a doctor realizes that she's feeling irritated, for instance, that may be a signal that the patient is bothered too.

Those who are utterly at a loss may be able to prime emotional empathy essentially by faking it until they make it, Riess adds. If you act in a caring way—looking people in the eye and paying attention to their expressions, even when you don't particularly want to—you may start to feel more engaged.

What's more, some lab research suggests that the appropriate application of empathic concern is critical to making moral judgments. Brain scans have revealed that when volunteers listened to tales of people subjected to physical pain, their own brain centers for experiencing such pain lit up instantly. But if the story was about psychological suffering, the higher brain centers involved in empathic concern and compassion took longer to activate. Some time is needed to grasp the psychological and moral dimensions of a situation. The more distracted we are, the less we can cultivate the subtler forms of empathy and compassion.

Building relationships

People who lack social sensitivity are easy to spot—at least for other people. They are the clueless among us. The CFO who is technically competent but bullies some people, freezes out others, and plays favorites—but when you point out what he has just done, shifts the blame, gets angry, or thinks that you're the problem—is not trying to be a jerk; he's utterly unaware of his shortcomings.

When Empathy Needs to Be Controlled

GETTING A GRIP on our impulse to empathize with other people's feelings can help us make better decisions when someone's emotional flood threatens to overwhelm us.

Ordinarily, when we see someone pricked with a pin, our brains emit a signal indicating that our own pain centers are echoing that distress. But physicians learn in medical school to block even such automatic responses. Their attentional anesthetic seems to be deployed by the temporal-parietal junction and regions of the prefrontal cortex, a circuit that boosts concentration by tuning out emotions. That's what is happening in your brain when you distance yourself from others in order to stay calm and help them. The same neural network kicks in when we see a problem in an emotionally overheated environment and need to focus on looking for a solution. If you're talking with someone who is upset, this system helps you understand the person's perspective intellectually by shifting from the heart-to-heart of emotional empathy to the head-to-heart of cognitive empathy.

Social sensitivity appears to be related to cognitive empathy. Cognitively empathic executives do better at overseas assignments, for instance, presumably because they quickly pick up implicit norms and learn the unique mental models of a new culture. Attention to social context lets us act with skill no matter what the situation, instinctively follow the universal algorithm for etiquette, and behave in ways that put others at ease. (In another age this might have been called good manners.)

Circuitry that converges on the anterior hippocampus reads social context and leads us intuitively to act differently with, say, our college buddies than with our families or our colleagues. In concert with the deliberative prefrontal cortex, it squelches the impulse to do something inappropriate. Accordingly, one brain test for sensitivity to context assesses the function of the hippocampus. The University of Wisconsin neuroscientist Richard Davidson hypothesizes that people who are most alert to social situations exhibit stronger activity and more connections between the hippocampus and the prefrontal cortex than those who just can't seem to get it right.

The same circuits may be at play when we map social networks in a group—a skill that lets us navigate the relationships in those networks well. People who excel at organizational influence can not only sense the flow of personal connections but also name the people whose opinions hold most sway, and so focus on persuading those who will persuade others.

Alarmingly, research suggests that as people rise through the ranks and gain power, their ability to perceive and maintain personal connections tends to suffer a sort of psychic attrition. In studying encounters between people of varying status, Dacher Keltner, a psychologist at Berkeley, has found that higher-ranking individuals consistently focus their gaze less on lower-ranking people and are more likely to interrupt or to monopolize the conversation.

In fact, mapping attention to power in an organization gives a clear indication of hierarchy: The longer it takes Person A to respond to Person B, the more relative power Person A has. Map response times across an entire organization, and you'll get a remarkably accurate chart of social standing. The boss leaves e-mails unanswered for hours; those lower down respond within minutes. This is so predictable that an algorithm for it—called automated social hierarchy detection—has been developed at Columbia University. Intelligence agencies reportedly are applying the algorithm to suspected terrorist gangs to piece together chains of influence and identify central figures.

But the real point is this: Where we see ourselves on the social ladder sets the default for how much attention we pay. This should be a warning to top executives, who need to respond to fast-moving competitive situations by tapping the full range of ideas and talents within an organization. Without a deliberate shift in attention, their natural inclination may be to ignore smart ideas from the lower ranks.

Focusing on the Wider World

Leaders with a strong outward focus are not only good listeners but also good questioners. They are visionaries who can sense the far-flung consequences of local decisions and imagine how the choices they make today will play out in the future. They are open to the surprising ways in which seemingly unrelated data can inform their central interests. Melinda Gates offered up a cogent example when she remarked on *60 Minutes* that her husband was the kind of person who would read an entire book about fertilizer. Charlie Rose asked, Why fertilizer? The connection was obvious to Bill Gates, who is constantly looking for technological advances that can save lives on a massive scale. "A few billion people would have to die if we hadn't come up with fertilizer," he replied.

Focusing on strategy

Any business school course on strategy will give you the two main elements: exploitation of your current advantage and exploration for new ones. Brain scans that were performed on 63 seasoned business decision makers as they pursued or switched between exploitative and exploratory strategies revealed the specific circuits involved. Not surprisingly, exploitation requires concentration on the job at hand, whereas exploration demands open awareness to recognize new possibilities. But exploitation is accompanied by activity in the brain's circuitry for anticipation and reward. In other words, it feels good to coast along in a familiar routine. When we switch to exploration, we have to make a deliberate cognitive effort to disengage from that routine in order to roam widely and pursue fresh paths.

What keeps us from making that effort? Sleep deprivation, drinking, stress, and mental overload all interfere with the executive circuitry used to make the cognitive switch. To sustain the outward focus that leads to innovation, we need some uninterrupted time in which to reflect and refresh our focus.

The wellsprings of innovation

In an era when almost everyone has access to the same information, new value arises from putting ideas together in novel ways and asking smart questions that open up untapped potential. Moments before we have a creative insight, the brain shows a third-of-a-second spike in gamma waves, indicating the synchrony of far-flung brain cells. The more neurons firing in sync, the bigger the spike. Its timing suggests that what's happening is the formation of a new neural network—presumably creating a fresh association.

But it would be making too much of this to see gamma waves as a secret to creativity. A classic model of creativity suggests how the various modes of attention play key roles. First we prepare our minds by gathering a wide variety of pertinent information, and then we alternate between concentrating intently on the problem and letting our minds wander freely. Those activities translate roughly into vigilance, when while immersing ourselves in all kinds of input, we remain alert for anything relevant to the problem at hand; selective attention to the specific creative challenge; and open awareness, in which we allow our minds to associate freely and the solution to emerge spontaneously. (That's why so many fresh ideas come to people in the shower or out for a walk or a run.)

The dubious gift of systems awareness

If people are given a quick view of a photo of lots of dots and asked to guess how many there are, the strong systems thinkers in the group tend to make the best estimates. This skill shows up in those who are good at designing software, assembly lines, matrix organizations, or interventions to save failing ecosystems—it's a very powerful gift indeed. After all, we live within extremely complex systems. But, suggests the Cambridge University psychologist Simon Baron-Cohen (a cousin of Sacha's), in a small but significant number of people, a strong systems awareness is coupled with an empathy deficit—a blind spot for what other people are thinking and feeling and for reading social situations. For that reason, although people with a superior systems understanding are organizational assets, they are not necessarily effective leaders.

An executive at one bank explained to me that it has created a separate career ladder for systems analysts so that they can progress in status and salary on the basis of their systems smarts alone. That way, the bank can consult them as needed while recruiting leaders from a different pool—one containing people with emotional intelligence.

Putting It All Together

For those who don't want to end up similarly compartmentalized, the message is clear. A focused leader is not the person concentrating on the three most important priorities of the year, or the most brilliant systems thinker, or the one most in tune with the corporate culture. Focused leaders can command the full range of their own attention: They are in touch with their inner feelings, they can control their impulses, they are aware of how others see them, they understand what others need from them, they can weed out distractions and also allow their minds to roam widely, free of preconceptions.

This is challenging. But if great leadership were a paint-by-numbers exercise, great leaders would be more common. Practically every form of focus can be strengthened. What it takes is not talent so much as diligence—a willingness to exercise the attention circuits of the brain just as we exercise our analytic skills and other systems of the body.

The link between attention and excellence remains hidden most of the time. Yet attention is the basis of the most essential of leadership skills—emotional, organizational, and strategic intelligence. And never has it been under greater assault. The constant onslaught of incoming data leads to sloppy shortcuts—triaging our e-mail by reading only the subject lines, skipping many of our voice mails, skimming memos and reports. Not only do our habits of attention make us less effective, but the sheer volume of all those messages leaves us too little time to reflect on what they really mean. This was foreseen more than 40 years ago by the Nobel Prize–winning economist Herbert Simon. Information "consumes the attention of its recipients," he wrote in 1971. "Hence a wealth of information creates a poverty of attention."

My goal here is to place attention center stage so that you can direct it where you need it when you need it. Learn to master your attention, and you will be in command of where you, and your organization, focus.

Originally published in December 2013. Reprint R1312B

The Big Lie of Strategic Planning

by Roger L. Martin

ALL EXECUTIVES KNOW that strategy is important. But almost all also find it scary, because it forces them to confront a future they can only guess at. Worse, actually choosing a strategy entails making decisions that explicitly cut off possibilities and options. An executive may well fear that getting those decisions wrong will wreck his or her career.

The natural reaction is to make the challenge less daunting by turning it into a problem that can be solved with tried and tested tools. That nearly always means spending weeks or even months preparing a comprehensive plan for how the company will invest in existing and new assets and capabilities in order to achieve a target—an increased share of the market, say, or a share in some new one. The plan is typically supported with detailed spreadsheets that project costs and revenue quite far into the future. By the end of the process, everyone feels a lot less scared.

This is a truly terrible way to make strategy. It may be an excellent way to cope with fear of the unknown, but fear and discomfort are an essential part of strategy making. In fact, if you are entirely comfortable with your strategy, there's a strong chance it isn't very good. You're probably stuck in one or more of the traps I'll discuss in this article. You need to be uncomfortable and apprehensive: True strategy is about placing bets and making hard choices. The objective is not to eliminate risk but to increase the odds of success.

49

In this worldview, managers accept that good strategy is not the product of hours of careful research and modeling that lead to an inevitable and almost perfect conclusion. Instead, it's the result of a simple and quite rough-and-ready process of thinking through what it would take to achieve what you want and then assessing whether it's realistic to try. If executives adopt this definition, then maybe, just maybe, they can keep strategy where it should be: outside the comfort zone.

Comfort Trap 1: Strategic Planning

Virtually every time the word "strategy" is used, it is paired with some form of the word "plan," as in the process of "strategic planning" or the resulting "strategic plan." The subtle slide from strategy to planning occurs because planning is a thoroughly doable and comfortable exercise.

Strategic plans all tend to look pretty much the same. They usually have three major parts. The first is a vision or mission statement that sets out a relatively lofty and aspirational goal. The second is a list of initiatives—such as product launches, geographic expansions, and construction projects—that the organization will carry out in pursuit of the goal. This part of the strategic plan tends to be very organized but also very long. The length of the list is generally constrained only by affordability.

The third element is the conversion of the initiatives into financials. In this way, the plan dovetails nicely with the annual budget. Strategic plans become the budget's descriptive front end, often projecting five years of financials in order to appear "strategic." But management typically commits only to year one; in the context of years two through five, "strategic" actually means "impressionistic."

This exercise arguably makes for more thoughtful and thorough budgets. However, it must not be confused with strategy. Planning typically isn't explicit about what the organization chooses not to do and why. It does not question assumptions. And its dominant logic is affordability; the plan consists of whichever initiatives fit the company's resources.

THE BIG LIE OF STRATEGIC PLANNING

Idea in Brief

The Problem

In an effort to get a handle on strategy, managers spend thousands of hours drawing up detailed plans that project revenue far into the future. These plans may make managers feel good, but all too often they matter very little to performance.

Why It Happens

Strategy making is uncomfortable; it's about taking risks and facing the unknown. Unsurprisingly, managers try to turn it into a comfortable set of activities. But reassurance won't deliver performance.

The Solution

Reconcile yourself to feeling uncomfortable, and follow three rules:

Keep it simple. Capture your strategy in a one-pager that addresses where you will play and how you will win.

Don't look for perfection. Strategy isn't about finding answers. It's about placing bets and shortening odds.

Make the logic explicit. Be clear about what must change for you to achieve your strategic goal.

Mistaking planning for strategy is a common trap. Even board members, who are supposed to be keeping managers honest about strategy, fall into it. They are, after all, primarily current or former managers, who find it safer to supervise planning than to encourage strategic choice. Moreover, Wall Street is more interested in the short-term goals described in plans than in the long-term goals that are the focus of strategy. Analysts pore over plans in order to assess whether companies can meet their quarterly goals.

Comfort Trap 2: Cost-Based Thinking

The focus on planning leads seamlessly to cost-based thinking. Costs lend themselves wonderfully to planning, because by and large they are under the control of the company. For the vast majority of costs, the company plays the role of customer. It decides how many employees to hire, how many square feet of real estate to lease, how many machines to procure, how much advertising to air, and so on. In some cases a company can, like any customer, decide to stop buying a particular good or service, and so even severance or shutdown costs can be under its control. Of course there are exceptions. Government agencies tell companies that they need to remit payroll taxes for each employee and buy a certain amount of compliance services. But the proverbial exceptions prove the rule: Costs imposed on the company by others make up a relatively small fraction of the overall cost picture, and most are derivative of company-controlled costs. (Payroll taxes, for instance, are incurred only when the company decides to hire an employee.)

Costs are comfortable because they can be planned for with relative precision. This is an important and useful exercise. Many companies are damaged or destroyed when they let their costs get out of control. The trouble is that planning-oriented managers tend to apply familiar, comfortable cost-side approaches to the revenue side as well, treating revenue planning as virtually identical to cost planning and as an equal component of the overall plan and budget. All too often, the result is painstaking work to build up revenue plans salesperson by salesperson, product by product, channel by channel, region by region.

But when the planned revenue doesn't show up, managers feel confused and even aggrieved. "What more could we have done?" they wonder. "We spent thousands upon thousands of hours planning."

There's a simple reason why revenue planning doesn't have the same desired result as cost planning. For costs, the company makes the decisions. But for revenue, customers are in charge. Except in the rare case of monopolies, customers can decide of their own free will whether to give revenue to the company, to its competitors, or to no one at all. Companies may fool themselves into thinking that revenue is under their control, but because it is neither knowable nor controllable, planning, budgeting, and forecasting it is an impressionistic exercise.

Of course, shorter-term revenue planning is much easier for companies that have long-term contracts with customers. For example, for business information provider Thomson Reuters, the bulk of its revenue each year comes from multiyear subscriptions. The only variable amount in the revenue plan is the difference between new

Giant Opportunities Encourage Bad Strategy

COMPANIES IN MANY INDUSTRIES prefer a small slice of a huge market to a large slice of a small one. The thinking is, of course, that the former promises unlimited growth potential. And there's a certain amount of truth to that. But all too often, the size of the opportunity encourages sloppy strategy making. Why choose where to play or how to win when there's a huge market to conquer? Anybody is a potential customer, so just go out and sell stuff.

But when anyone could be a customer, it is impossible to figure out whom to target and what those people actually want. The results tend to be an offering that is not captivating to anybody and a sales force that doesn't know where to spend its time. This is when crisp strategy making and clear thinking about opportunities are most important.

When you're facing a huge growth opportunity, it is smarter to think sequentially: Determine what piece of the overall market to tackle first and target it precisely and relentlessly. Once you've achieved a dominant position in that segment, expand from there into the next, and so on.

---

subscription sales and cancellations at the end of existing contracts. Similarly, if a company has long order backlogs, as Boeing does, it will be able to predict revenue more accurately, although the Boeing Dreamliner tribulations demonstrate that even "firm orders" don't automatically translate into future revenue. Over the longer term, all revenue is controlled by the customer.

The bottom line, therefore, is that the predictability of costs is fundamentally different from the predictability of revenue. Planning can't and won't make revenue magically appear, and the effort you spend creating revenue plans is a distraction from the strategist's much harder job: finding ways to acquire and keep customers.

Comfort Trap 3: Self-Referential Strategy Frameworks

This trap is perhaps the most insidious, because it can snare even managers who, having successfully avoided the planning and cost traps, are trying to build a real strategy. In identifying and articulating a strategy, most executives adopt one of a number of standard frameworks. Unfortunately, two of the most popular ones can lead the unwary user to design a strategy entirely around what the company can control.

In 1978 Henry Mintzberg published an influential article in *Management Science* that introduced *emergent strategy,* a concept he later popularized for the wider nonacademic business audience in his successful 1994 book, *The Rise and Fall of Strategic Planning.* Mintzberg's insight was simple but indeed powerful. He distinguished between *deliberate strategy,* which is intentional, and emergent strategy, which is not based on an original intention but instead consists of the company's responses to a variety of unanticipated events.

Mintzberg's thinking was informed by his observation that managers overestimate their ability to predict the future and to plan for it in a precise and technocratic way. By drawing a distinction between deliberate and emergent strategy, he wanted to encourage managers to watch carefully for changes in their environment and make course corrections in their deliberate strategy accordingly. In addition, he warned against the dangers of sticking to a fixed strategy in the face of substantial changes in the competitive environment.

All of this is eminently sensible advice that every manager would be wise to follow. However, most managers do not. Instead, most use the idea that a strategy emerges as events unfold as a justification for declaring the future to be so unpredictable and volatile that it doesn't make sense to make strategy choices until the future becomes sufficiently clear. Notice how comforting that interpretation is: No longer is there a need to make angst-ridden decisions about unknowable and uncontrollable things.

A little digging into the logic reveals some dangerous flaws in it. If the future is too unpredictable and volatile to make strategic choices, what would lead a manager to believe that it will become significantly less so? And how would that manager recognize the point when predictability is high enough and volatility is low enough to start making choices? Of course the premise is

Are You Stuck in the Comfort Zone?

Probably

- You have a large corporate strategic planning group.
- In addition to profit, your most important performance metrics are cost- and capabilities-based.
- Strategy is presented to the board by your strategic planning staff.
- Board members insist on proof that the strategy will succeed before approving it.

Probably Not

- If you have a corporate strategy group, it is tiny.
- In addition to profit, your most important performance metrics are customer satisfaction and market share.
- Strategy is presented to the board primarily by line executives.
- Board members ask for a thorough description of the risks involved in a strategy before approving it.

---

untenable: There won't be a time when anyone can be sure that the future is predictable.

Hence, the concept of emergent strategy has simply become a handy excuse for avoiding difficult strategic choices, for replicating as a "fast follower" the choices that appear to be succeeding for others, and for deflecting any criticism for not setting out in a bold direction. Simply following competitors' choices will never produce a unique or valuable advantage. None of this is what Mintzberg intended, but it is a common outcome of his framework, because it plays into managers' comfort zone.

In 1984, six years after Mintzberg's original article introducing emergent strategy, Birger Wernerfelt wrote "A Resource-Based View of the Firm," which put forth another enthusiastically embraced concept in strategy. But it wasn't until 1990, when C.K. Prahalad and Gary Hamel wrote one of the most widely read HBR articles of all time, "The Core Competence of the Corporation," that Wernerfelt's resource-based view (RBV) of the firm was widely popularized with managers.

RBV holds that the key to a firm's competitive advantage is the possession of valuable, rare, inimitable, and non-substitutable capabilities. This concept became extraordinarily appealing to executives, because it seemed to suggest that strategy was the identification and building of "core competencies," or "strategic capabilities." Note that this conveniently falls within the realm of the knowable and controllable. Any company can build a technical sales force or a software development lab or a distribution network and declare it a core competence. Executives can comfortably invest in such capabilities and control the entire experience. Within reason, they can guarantee success.

The problem, of course, is that capabilities themselves don't compel a customer to buy. Only those that produce a superior value equation for a particular set of customers can do that. But customers and context are both unknowable and uncontrollable. Many executives prefer to focus on capabilities that can be built—for certain. And if those don't produce success, capricious customers or irrational competitors can take the blame.

Escaping the Traps

It's easy to identify companies that have fallen into these traps. (See "Are You Stuck in the Comfort Zone?") In those companies, boards tend to be highly comfortable with the planners and spend lots of time reviewing and approving their work. Discussion in management and board meetings tends to focus on how to squeeze more profit out of existing revenue rather than how to generate new revenue. The principal metrics concern finance and capabilities; those that deal with customer satisfaction or market share (especially changes in the latter) take the backseat.

How can a company escape those traps? Because the problem is rooted in people's natural aversion to discomfort and fear, the only remedy is to adopt a discipline about strategy making that reconciles you to experiencing some angst. This involves ensuring that the strategy-making process conforms to three basic rules. Keeping to the rules isn't easy—the comfort zone is always alluring—and it won't necessarily result in a successful strategy. But if you can follow them, you will at least be sure that your strategy won't be a bad one.

Rule 1: Keep the strategy statement simple

Focus your energy on the key choices that influence revenue decision makers—that is, customers. They will decide to spend their money with your company if your value proposition is superior to competitors'. Two choices determine success: the where-to-play decision (which specific customers to target) and the how-to-win decision (how to create a compelling value proposition for those customers). If a customer is not in the segment or area where the company chooses to play, she probably won't even become aware of the availability and nature of its offering. If the company does connect with that customer, the how-to-win choice will determine whether she will find the offering's targeted value equation compelling.

If a strategy is about just those two decisions, it won't need to involve the production of long and tedious planning documents. There is no reason why a company's strategy choices can't be summarized in one page with simple words and concepts. Characterizing the key choices as where to play and how to win keeps the discussion grounded and makes it more likely that managers will engage with the strategic challenges the firm faces rather than retreat to their planning comfort zone.

Rule 2: Recognize that strategy is not about perfection

As noted, managers unconsciously feel that strategy should achieve the accuracy and predictive power of cost planning—in other words, it should be nearly perfect. But given that strategy is primarily about revenue rather than cost, perfection is an impossible standard. At its very best, therefore, strategy shortens the odds of a company's bets. Managers must internalize that fact if they are not to be intimidated by the strategy-making process.

For that to happen, boards and regulators need to reinforce rather than undermine the notion that strategy involves a bet. Every time a board asks managers if they are sure about their strategy or regulators make them certify the thoroughness of their strategy decision-making processes, it weakens actual strategy making. As much as boards

57

and regulators may want the world to be knowable and controllable, that's simply not how it works. Until they accept this, they will get planning instead of strategy—and lots of excuses down the line about why the revenue didn't show up.

Rule 3: Make the logic explicit

The only sure way to improve the hit rate of your strategic choices is to test the logic of your thinking: For your choices to make sense, what do you need to believe about customers, about the evolution of your industry, about competition, about your capabilities? It is critical to write down the answers to those questions, because the human mind naturally rewrites history and will declare the world to have unfolded largely as was planned rather than recall how strategic bets were actually made and why. If the logic is recorded and then compared to real events, managers will be able to see quickly when and how the strategy is not producing the desired outcome and will be able to make necessary adjustments—just as Henry Mintzberg envisioned. In addition, by observing with some level of rigor what works and what doesn't, managers will be able to improve their strategy decision making.

As managers apply these rules, their fear of making strategic choices will diminish. That's good—but only up to a point. If a company is completely comfortable with its choices, it's at risk of missing important changes in its environment.

———————

I have argued that planning, cost management, and focusing on capabilities are dangerous traps for the strategy maker. Yet those activities are essential; no company can neglect them. For if it's strategy that compels customers to give the company its revenue, planning, cost control, and capabilities determine whether the revenue can be obtained at a price that is profitable for the company. Human nature being what it is, though, planning and the other activities will always dominate strategy rather than serve it—unless a conscious effort is made to prevent that. If you are comfortable with your company's strategy, chances are you're probably not making that effort.

Originally published in January–February 2014. Reprint R1401F

Contextual Intelligence

by Tarun Khanna

WHETHER AS MANAGERS or as academics, we study business to extract learning, formalize it, and apply it to puzzles we wish to solve.
That's why we go to business school, why we write case studies and
develop analytic frameworks, why we read HBR.

I believe deeply in the importance of that work: I've spent my career studying business as it is practiced in varied global settings.

But I've come to a conclusion that may surprise you: Trying
to apply management practices uniformly across geographies is
a fool's errand, much as we'd like to think otherwise. To be sure,
plenty of aspirations enjoy wide if not universal acceptance. Most
entrepreneurs and managers agree, for example, that creating value
and motivating talent are at the heart of what they do. But once
you drill below the homilies, differences quickly emerge over what
constitutes value and how to motivate people. That's because conditions differ enormously from place to place, in ways that aren't
easy to codify—conditions not just of economic development but of
institutional character, physical geography, educational norms, language, and culture. Students of management once thought that best
manufacturing practices (to take one example) were sufficiently
established that processes merely needed tweaking to fit local conditions. More often, it turns out, they need radical reworking—not

because the technology is wrong but because everything surrounding the technology changes how it will work.

It's not that we're ignoring the problem—not at all. Business schools increasingly offer opportunities for students and managers to study practices abroad. At Harvard Business School, where I teach, international research is essential to our mission, and we now send first-year MBA students out into the world to briefly experience the challenges local businesses face. Nonetheless, I continually find that people overestimate what they know about how to succeed in other countries.

Context matters. This is not news to social scientists, or indeed to my colleagues who study leadership, but we have paid it insufficient attention in the field of management. There is nothing wrong with the analytic tools we have at our disposal, but their application requires careful thought. It requires *contextual intelligence:* the ability to understand the limits of our knowledge and to adapt that knowledge to an environment different from the one in which it was developed. (The term is not new; my HBS colleagues Anthony Mayo and Nitin Nohria have recently used it in the pages of HBR, and academic references date from the mid-1980s.) Until we acquire and apply this kind of intelligence, the failure rate for cross-border businesses will remain high, our ability to learn from experiments unfolding across the globe will remain limited, and the promise of healthy growth worldwide will remain unfulfilled.

Why Knowledge Often Doesn't Cross Borders

I started thinking about contextual intelligence some years ago, when my colleague Jan Rivkin and I studied how profitable different industries were in various countries. To say that what we found surprised us would be an understatement.

First some background. Into the 1990s, empirical economists studying the economies of the OECD member countries, whose data were readily available, concluded that similar industries tended to have similar structures and deliver similar economic returns. This led to a widespread assumption that a given industry would be

Idea in Brief

The Finding

Most universal truths about management play out differently in different contexts: Best practices don't necessarily travel.

The Implications

Global companies won't succeed in unfamiliar markets unless they adapt—or even rebuild—their operating models.

The Solution

The first steps in that adaptation are the toughest: jettisoning assumptions about what will work and then experimenting to find out what actually does work.

just as profitable or unprofitable in any country—and that industry analysis, one of the most rigorous tools we have, would support that assumption. But when data from multiple *non*-OECD countries became available, we could not replicate those results. Knowing something about the performance of a particular industry in one country was no guarantee that we could predict its structure or returns elsewhere. (See the sidebar "How Well Correlated Is Industry Profitability Across Countries?")

To see why performance might vary so much, consider the cement industry. The technology for manufacturing cement is similar everywhere, but individual cement plants are located within specific contexts that vary widely. Corrupt materials suppliers may adulterate the mixtures that go into cement. Unions may support or impede plant operations. Finished cement may be sold to construction firms in bulk or to individuals in bags. Such variables often outweigh the unifying effect of a common technology. A cement plant manager moving to an unfamiliar setting would indeed have a leg up on someone who had never managed such a plant before, but not by nearly as much as she might think.

Rather than assume that technical knowledge will trump local conditions, we should expect *institutional context* to significantly affect industry structure. Each of Michael Porter's five forces (which together describe industry structure) is influenced by local institutions, such as those that enforce contracts and provide capital. In a country where only established players have access to these,

How Well Correlated Is Industry Profitability Across Countries?

by Tarun Khanna and Jan W. Rivkin

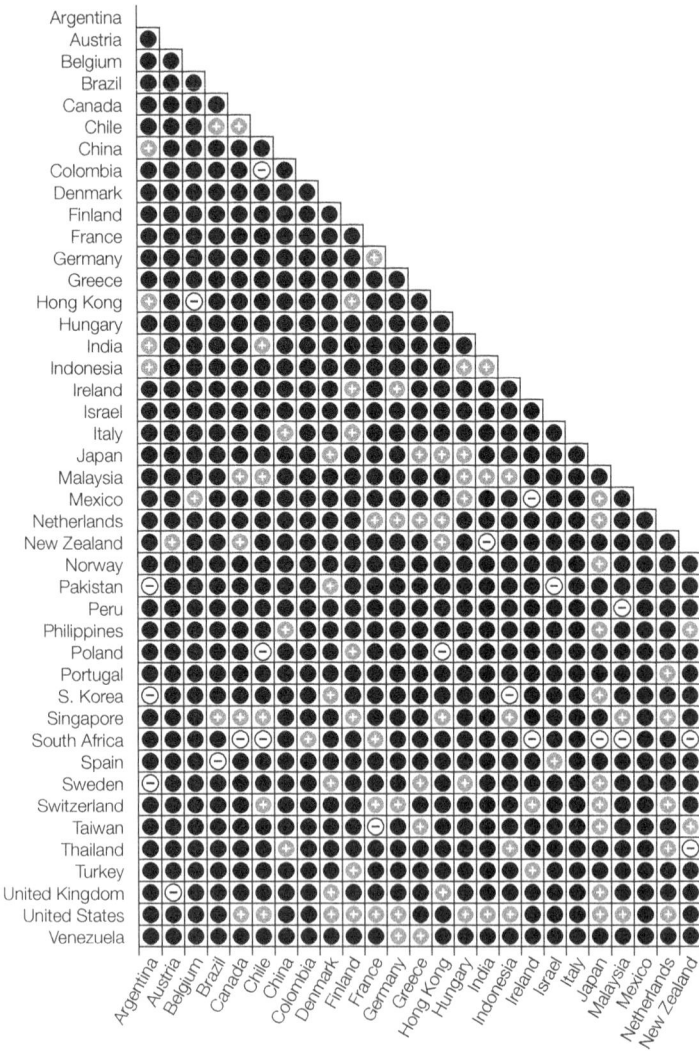

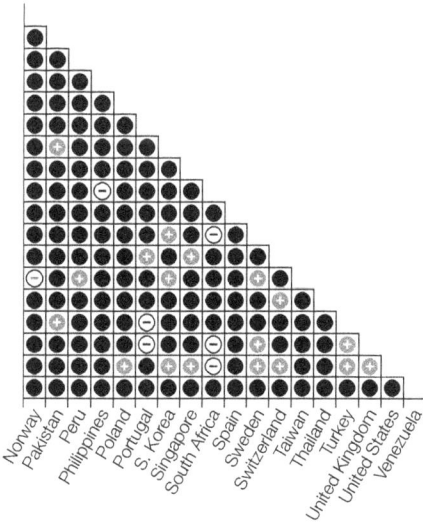

Positive correlation
Significant at the 10% level

Insignificant correlation

Negative correlation
Significant at the 10% level

(continued)

How Well Correlated Is Industry Profitability Across Countries?

(continued)

UNTIL RECENTLY, MANY STRATEGISTS believed that patterns of profitability in developed countries would show up in less developed economies as well. They couldn't know for sure, because empirical research on business strategy had focused on a small handful of advanced economies. But it was often assumed that if an industry was highly profitable in, say, Germany, it would also be highly profitable in Thailand or Brazil.

In 2001, as good data on emerging markets started to become available, we checked that assumption by computing the average profitability of individual industries in each of 43 countries and checking correlation between the countries in every pairing.

If it were indeed true that profitability is predictable from country to country, most of this chart would be dark gray, reflecting significant positive correlation (meaning that industries profitable in one country are likely to be so in

incumbent cement producers can prevent the emergence of new rivals. That consolidation of power means they can keep prices high. To use the language of business strategists, the logic of how value is created and divided among industry participants is unchanged, but its application is constrained by contextual variables. The institutional context affects the cement maker's profitability far more than how good she is at producing cement.

Much of my academic work has focused on institutional context. With my colleague Krishna Palepu, I've explored the idea that developing countries typically lack the "specialized intermediaries" that allow new enterprises to reach a broad market: courts that adjudicate disputes, venture capitalists that lend money, accreditation agencies that corroborate claims, and so on. Over time these voids are filled by entrepreneurs and better-run governments, and eventually the country "emerges" with a formal economy that functions reasonably well. Our framework has proved useful to businesses and scholars trying to understand a particular country's institutional context and how to build a business within it. (Our book *Winning in* others, to a degree beyond the relationship prone to arise by chance). Such correlation, however, exists in only about 11% of cases, and it's often between similar nations—the United States and Canada, for example.

Instead the chart is dominated by black: There's no significant correlation of industry profitability between most of these country pairs. The fact that an industry is highly profitable in Sweden tells us nothing about whether it will be profitable in Singapore.

The implications are alarming. Companies enter new markets all the time relying on what they think they know about how their industry works and the technical competencies that have allowed them to succeed in their home markets. But given the results of our study, it's not much of a stretch to say that what you learn in your home market about a particular industry may have very little to do with what you'll need to succeed in a new market.

Emerging Markets: A Road Map for Strategy and Execution looks at institutional voids in more depth.)

Contextual intelligence requires moving far beyond an analysis of institutional context into areas as diverse as intellectual property rights, aesthetic preferences, attitudes toward power, beliefs about the free market, and even religious differences. The most difficult work is often the "soft" work of adjusting mental models, learning to differentiate between universal principles and their specific embodiments, and being open to new ideas.

Even Good Companies Have a Really Hard Time

Businesses that have achieved success in one market invariably have tightly woven operating models and highly disciplined cultures that fit that market's context—so they sometimes find it *more* difficult to pull those things apart and rebuild than other companies do. Shifting into a new context may be straightforward if just one or two parts of the model need to change. But generally the adaptations required are far more complicated than that. In addition, executives rarely understand precisely why their operating model works, which makes reverse engineering all the more difficult, even for highly successful companies.

Metro Cash & Carry, a big-box wholesaler that provides urban businesses with fresh foods and dry goods, illustrates this point well. Metro successfully expanded from Germany to other parts of Western Europe and then to Eastern Europe and Russia, learning from each experience. So when the company entered the Chinese market, Metro executives knew they'd have to make adjustments but assumed that their basic recipe for success, tempered by what they'd learned, was transferable. They did indeed get a lot right, partly by developing effective partnerships and partly by helping provincial governments experiment with advanced food-safety techniques.

Nonetheless, the company ran into multiple challenges it had not fully anticipated. In any given location in China, learning how to work with the constellation of political and economic players took months. Lessons learned in one place often didn't transfer to other places. Local competition was tougher overall than it had been in Eastern Europe and Russia (which Metro entered in an era of generalized scarcity, in the years after the Berlin Wall came down). Metro managers, who were used to large, formal competitors, experienced the multiplicity of agile rivals in the informal economy as almost a "fog of war." Other challenges resulted from local tastes: Many consumers preferred to buy live or freshly butchered animals from wet markets, for example. As a result of these difficulties, the company didn't break even in China until 2008—14 years after entering the market.

India turned out to be even tougher, although Metro had good reasons for optimism: It saw a way to cut out middlemen and thereby lower prices. It offered high-quality, standardized products in an environment with endemic food-quality and hygiene problems and staggering waste. Its wide assortment of goods seemed sure to appeal to its target customers—mom-and-pop retailers, which are so tightly packed together that India has the highest retailer density per capita in the world.

Still, Metro confronted obstacles different from those it had encountered in other markets. It had trouble getting around an anachronistic law that required farmers to sell all produce through government-run auctions. Traders and retailers that Metro thought would benefit from its presence put up raucous resistance. And for the first time in the company's experience, no one seemed to be in charge: Metro couldn't find a single-point political authority willing to advocate for it. In addition, its Indian customers were used to informal sources of credit and found it inconvenient to carry away wholesale quantities of goods and produce, owing to India's dilapidated infrastructure.

Metro's managers took a long time to understand that their model had to change, but they never really contemplated giving up. Just because a company is "global," however, doesn't mean it should do business in every country. Sometimes the amount of adaptation needed is so great that its core operating model would fall apart. Though Metro ultimately created *more* value in India than elsewhere, I believe, it did so only after very slow experimentation. This was partly because whatever adaptations the local team proposed and headquarters approved had to unfold in the context of an undisciplined political process and constant shrill criticism from unfamiliar media, often in the vernacular. Also, organizational rigidity had inevitably set in, stemming from individual managers' overconfidence in the formula for past successes. Metro's managers are first-rate, but contextual intelligence can't be rushed or mandated into existence.

The difficulties I describe aren't peculiar to developed-country companies trying to enter emerging markets. Metro's tribulations in India, for example, resemble those that organized commerce faced with the Poujadism of 1950s France, when mom-and-pop businesses were up in arms against the establishment. Germany encountered similar forces in that period. And developing-economy enterprises trying to move into first-world markets have to change their operating models, too. Whereas at home they may have succeeded by managing around—or taking advantage of—conditions such as a cash-only society, intrusive or corrupt government officials, and a shortage of talent, they face different challenges in developed markets.

Narayana Health, founded in Bangalore, is an example. Its famous cardiac-surgery group performs 12% of the heart operations done in India each year. CABG (coronary artery bypass graft) surgery costs the patient as little as $2,000, compared with $60,000 to $100,000 in the United States, yet Narayana's mortality and infection rates are the same as those of its U.S. counterparts. Still, it's unclear whether the group's operating model will transfer easily to the Cayman Islands, where Narayana opened a facility in February 2014. Why? Because it achieved success under specifically Indian conditions: A huge number of patients need the surgery, which means that surgeons quickly acquire expertise and thereby reduce costs. Having to overcome the logistical, financial, and behavioral barriers that kept poor patients away taught valuable lessons. Nurses double as respiratory and occupational therapists, and family members are now enlisted to help provide postoperative care. In addition, construction materials are inexpensive and the loose regulatory culture allows for experimentation. In the Caymans, Narayana will inevitably have to pull apart this operating model, and a coherent replacement will emerge only gradually.

Some early signs are encouraging. The Caymans' material and labor costs are higher than India's, but construction practices honed at home have already allowed Narayana to build a state-of-the-art hospital in the islands for much less than it would have cost in most Western locations. The health group has another big thing going for it: Its culture has been one of experimentation from the beginning. The Caymans' very different regulatory systems will limit innovation in health care delivery methods, but an ingrained habit of questioning assumptions, trying out new approaches, and adjusting them in real time should serve Narayana well as it adapts.

How Can We Get Better at This?

Some of the ways to acquire contextual intelligence are obvious, though they're neither easy nor cheap: hiring people who are "fluent" in more than one culture; partnering with local companies;

developing local talent; doing more fieldwork and more cross-disciplinary work in business schools and requiring students to do the same; and taking the time to understand the nature and range of local variations. (See the sidebar "Tuning In to Cultural Differences.") Exploring all those approaches in detail is beyond the scope of this article, but I'd like to highlight a few perhaps less obvious points.

The "hard" stuff is easy (believe it or not)

Once you accept up front that you know less than you think you do, and that your operating model will have to change significantly in new markets, researching a country's institutional context isn't difficult—in fact, general information is usually available. It can be helpful to work from a road map or a checklist, which will help you recognize and then categorize unfamiliar phenomena. (*Winning in Emerging Markets* provides a tool for spotting institutional voids along with checklists on product, labor, and capital markets in emerging economies.) The institutional context should influence not just your industry analysis but any other strategic tools you typically use: break-even analysis, identification of key corporate resources, and so on.

One big caveat: Developing economies often lack the data sources—credit registries, market research firms, financial analysts—that managers in OECD countries take for granted. This absence creates an institutional void in developing economies that companies must fill through investments of their own. HSBC partnered with a local retailer to create Poland's first credit registry, for example, and Citibank did something similar in India as part of its effort to introduce credit cards there.

The soft stuff is hard

We tend to have very persistent mental models, particularly about emerging markets, that are not rooted in the facts and that get in the way of progress. One of these is the view that all countries will eventually converge on a free-market economy. But considerable evidence suggests that state-managed markets like China's will be with us for the foreseeable future. I've written elsewhere that the Chinese

Tuning In to Cultural Differences

UNDERSTANDING LOCAL VARIATIONS involves observing both customers and employees. On the "buy" side, differing aesthetic tastes aren't immediately apparent to many managers, but they matter a lot.

To succeed in India, Metro Cash & Carry increased the visual density of its stores' previously uncluttered aisles so that they would more closely resemble crowded Indian street markets. In contrast, eBay stuck with its U.S. playbook in China, allowing Taobao to win the Chinese market in less than three years; the upstart succeeded in part by capitalizing on local responsiveness to colorful, active websites.

Computer scientists and cognitive psychologists have demonstrated that different cultural groups have differing tastes in how information and products are represented. (An interactive at labinthewild.org allows you to compare your engagement style with that of diverse other respondents.)

Tastes also differ in luxury services; for instance, hotel room décor that appeals to one set of customers may alienate another. Artwork evoking England in its imperial age may be pleasing in York but irritating in Mumbai. Chinese executives accustomed to celebratory red-and-gold furnishings may perceive modernist minimalism in their Berlin or New York hotel rooms as cold and hostile. Religious imagery is similarly controversial: The Hindu goddess of wealth is often used to connect products to prosperity in India, whereas companies in the West rarely use religious iconography to market their wares.

Advertising agencies must work with different manifestations of universal values all the time. Bartle Bogle Hegarty's campaign for Johnnie Walker scotch whisky, for example, sought to link the product to the notion of a continual quest for self-improvement, which research had shown was the most powerful indicator of eventual male success. The iconic brand emblem—a striding man—embodied the idea that one should "keep walking." But what worked in the West—ads that focused on individual progress—failed in China and Thailand, where customers responded instead to evocations of camaraderie, shared commitment, and collective advancement. (One of the creative leads of the campaign speculated with me recently that the man's striding from left to right might well play differently in societies that write from right to left.)

On the "sell" side, managers must evaluate how to align incentives, motivation, and retention policies with local norms and expectations. If a country lacks efficient stock markets, for example, making stock options part of a compensation package becomes problematic. Similarly, individualized compensation schemes may be ineffective in an environment where collectivist values dominate.

government is the entrepreneur in that economy; to automatically equate governmental ubiquity with inefficiency, as we often do in the West, is wrong. A second persistent mind-set is the impulse to rely on simple explanations for complex phenomena. Metro's managers were slow to reconceptualize their operating model in part because they found it easier to address one factor at a time and hope to be done with it. (I see this problem in my classes all the time—sophisticated executives read a case and home in on one particular difficulty, whereas in reality a constellation of intersecting issues must be addressed.) Often the cognitive biases that Kahneman and Tversky first wrote about—such as anchoring and overconfidence—reinforce this tendency.

Experimentation is messy—and essential

It's not enough to identify which of our mental models and biases need to be jettisoned. We must develop new models and frameworks. They will of course be imperfect—but we can't build a better knowledge base without codifying what we learn along the way. And that requires even billion-dollar corporations to think like entrepreneurs—to create hypotheses about what will work, to document and test assumptions, and to experiment in order to learn, cheaply and quickly, what does or doesn't work. Like entrepreneurs, companies shouldn't analyze experimental results to the point of exhaustion but instead develop the capacity to act speedily on results.

General ideas travel; specific dimensions may not

Learning to distinguish between the two is key. (Once again, creating value and motivating the workforce are universally considered essential—but the meaning of "value" and the road to "motivation" differ enormously between cultures.) Metro has continued to define itself in the same way across borders: as a B2B wholesaler that gives small and midsize enterprises access to a diverse range of hard and soft goods. But major adjustments were needed to make that definition work in varying contexts. Regarding payment and delivery, for example, Metro learned to manage not just conventional cash-and-carry operations, but also cash-and-no-carry, carry-and-no-cash,

What's Universal? What's Context-Specific?

FIGURING OUT WHAT WILL TRAVEL from location to location and what won't is essential for nonprofits and fast-growing entrepreneurial ventures as well as for the established companies we've discussed here.

Consider Teach for America, a nonprofit started in the late 1980s, which helps talented college graduates spend a few years teaching in America's underperforming schools. It has recently mushroomed into a global network called Teach for All. The core ethos remains the same: Match willing, high-needs schools with recent graduates. But adapting the model requires a fair amount of contextual intelligence. Similarly, Aspiring Minds (of which I am a cofounder), an Indian talent-assessment service aimed at democratizing the market for talent, focuses on various out-of-the-mainstream job seekers in different markets.

ORGANIZATION Metro Cash & Carry	Teach for All	Aspiring Minds
TYPE Large, publicly traded company	Nonprofit	Entrepreneurial venture
SECTOR Wholesale	Education	Talent management
GEOGRAPHICAL SPREAD Germany to elsewhere in Europe, Russia, China, and India	U.S./UK to global	India to the U.S., the Middle East, and Africa
UNIVERSAL ATTRIBUTES Allows small and medium businesses (such as hoteliers, retailers, and caterers) to access a range of hard and soft goods	Matches accomplished but inexperienced would-be teachers with high-needs schools, over time nurturing a platform from which corporations can recruit talent	Helps mainstream corporations and out-of-the-mainstream job seekers find each other using state-of-the-art machine learning algorithms
CONTEXT-SPECIFIC ATTRIBUTES Provides multiple payment and delivery models: conventional cash-and-carry; cash plus delivery; credit plus carry; or credit plus delivery	Identifies high-needs schools in the education system; arranges funding in the absence of a culture of philanthropy; augments ordinary corporate recruiting	Identifies different types of job seekers, such as graduates of lesser-known schools, war veterans, and people educated online; adapts tools to reach and serve those pools

and no-cash-no-carry. (See "What's Universal? What's Context-Specific?")

The future can't be telescoped

We all tend to assume that social and economic transformations occur more quickly than they actually do. Some technological changes have an immediate impact (mobile phones have disseminated rapidly in emerging markets), but they are the exception. Robust research shows that countries take decades, on average, to adopt new technologies invented elsewhere. Institutional change is, if anything, even slower.

Research with my colleague Krishna Palepu suggests, for example, that the transition in Chile from a focus on bank loans to a focus on issuing securities (a key transition for entrepreneurship) took much longer than anticipated two decades ago. More was required than the creation of new organizations and new rules: Individuals had to adapt their behavior to the changed context. That didn't happen until foreign demand for information resulted in the emergence of local financial analysts and investment advisers, who first had to develop deep investing expertise. Similarly, in Korea the shift away from overreliance on bank debt and toward equity financing was far slower than proponents expected after the Asian financial crisis of the late 1990s. Analysts needed time to shed their biases, and it was difficult to locate truly independent directors.

For reasons akin to what we found in Chile and Korea, the harmonization of accounting, corporate governance, and intellectual property standards proceeds at a glacial pace relative to conventional managerial expectations—often because of political objections at the local level.

Generate your own data

To help focus on the facts as they are in a given context, rather than as managers think they should be, companies ought to obtain their own data whenever possible. This is particularly important when Western managers start to operate outside North America and Europe. What some scholars have called WEIRD (Western, educated, industrialized, rich, and democratic) societies may differ from the rest on a number of measures, including beliefs about fairness, a tendency to cooperate, the use of both inductive and moral reasoning, and concepts of self. Therefore, instead of hiring outsiders to do market research and assemble information on how other multinationals have entered a market, managers should conduct their own experiments to learn about the local context and what their company is capable of achieving within it. Some companies are experimenting with crowdsourcing data collection—a practice that's still in its infancy but showing real promise.

Be aware that context matters when eliciting information. In some settings community norms affect behavior more than individual-level incentives do. Thus a company interested in water conservation might learn more from studying how villagers use the communal well than from studying household water use. Focus groups may be ineffective in hierarchical societies, so it is important to figure out what "status" looks like in a given location.

Success requires patience

As noted, institutional change can't be rushed. Neither can enterprise-level change. Companies must be willing to invest in immersing their high-potential employees in particular local contexts. The global advertising giant WPP has a fellows program that places 10 recruits annually with its operating companies around the world to develop leaders with a multidisciplinary, culturally flexible perspective. Each fellow gains exposure and engagement while being mentored by senior WPP executives. Viewed as a ticket to success within the organization, the fellows program has resulted in 65% retention (over long time horizons) of these high-potential executives—a significant result in an industry notorious for turnover.

The Universal Importance of Contextual Intelligence

Understanding the limits of our knowledge, which is at the heart of contextual intelligence, is a very basic component of human comprehension. Yet it's also a profoundly difficult, complicated process that has vexed philosophers from Plato to Isaiah Berlin, who distinguished between *knowing the facts* and *making a judgment* in a widely read 1996 essay.

I believe that contextual intelligence is systematically undervalued in dozens of situations. I've focused here on corporations planning to enter new markets. I could as easily have written about giant state-owned enterprises, entrepreneurs, and nonprofits that are tackling even bigger problems—such as how to expand the formal economy to include the 4 billion people who currently make a living in the informal economy. At best, this excluded population engages in rudimentary commerce mediated by personal relationships, which limits the possibility of expanding its networks. Engaging effectively with this population will take massive doses of contextual intelligence. We need to understand so many things better than we currently do: How do they prioritize spending, given their extremely limited resources? What forms of communication will they respond to? How can they accumulate capital in the absence of collateral? The answers to those questions will differ from Mumbai to Nairobi and from Nairobi to Santiago.

Originally published in September 2014. Reprint R1409C

How Netflix Reinvented HR

by Patty McCord

SHERYL SANDBERG HAS CALLED it one of the most important documents ever to come out of Silicon Valley. It's been viewed more than 5 million times on the web. But when Reed Hastings and I (along with some colleagues) wrote a PowerPoint deck explaining how we shaped the culture and motivated performance at Netflix, where Hastings is CEO and I was chief talent officer from 1998 to 2012, we had no idea it would go viral. We realized that some of the talent management ideas we'd pioneered, such as the concept that workers should be allowed to take whatever vacation time they feel is appropriate, had been seen as a little crazy (at least until other companies started adopting them). But we were surprised that an unadorned set of 127 slides—no music, no animation—would become so influential.

People find the Netflix approach to talent and culture compelling for a few reasons. The most obvious one is that Netflix has been really successful: During 2013 alone its stock more than tripled, it won three Emmy awards, and its U.S. subscriber base grew to nearly 29 million. All that aside, the approach is compelling because it derives from common sense. In this article I'll go beyond the bullet points to describe five ideas that have defined the way Netflix attracts, retains, and manages talent. But first I'll share two conversations I had with early employees, both of which helped shape our overall philosophy.

The first took place in late 2001. Netflix had been growing quickly: We'd reached about 120 employees and had been planning an IPO. But after the dot-com bubble burst and the 9/11 attacks occurred, things changed. It became clear that we needed to put the IPO on hold and lay off a third of our employees. It was brutal. Then, a bit unexpectedly, DVD players became the hot gift that Christmas. By early 2002 our DVD-by-mail subscription business was growing like crazy. Suddenly we had far more work to do, with 30% fewer employees.

One day I was talking with one of our best engineers, an employee I'll call John. Before the layoffs, he'd managed three engineers, but now he was a one-man department working very long hours. I told John I hoped to hire some help for him soon. His response surprised me. "There's no rush—I'm happier now," he said. It turned out that the engineers we'd laid off weren't spectacular—they were merely adequate. John realized that he'd spent too much time riding herd on them and fixing their mistakes. "I've learned that I'd rather work by myself than with subpar performers," he said. His words echo in my mind whenever I describe the most basic element of Netflix's talent philosophy: The best thing you can do for employees—a perk better than foosball or free sushi—is hire only "A" players to work alongside them. Excellent colleagues trump everything else.

The second conversation took place in 2002, a few months after our IPO. Laura, our bookkeeper, was bright, hardworking, and creative. She'd been very important to our early growth, having devised a system for accurately tracking movie rentals so that we could pay the correct royalties. But now, as a public company, we needed CPAs and other fully credentialed, deeply experienced accounting professionals—and Laura had only an associate's degree from a community college. Despite her work ethic, her track record, and the fact that we all really liked her, her skills were no longer adequate. Some of us talked about jury-rigging a new role for her, but we decided that wouldn't be right.

So I sat down with Laura and explained the situation—and said that in light of her spectacular service, we would give her a spectacular severance package. I'd braced myself for tears or histrionics, but

Idea in Brief

The Idea

If a company hires correctly, workers will want to be star performers, and they can be managed through honest communication and common sense. Most companies focus too much on formal policies aimed at the small number of employees whose interests *aren't* fully aligned with the firm's.

The Solution

Hire, reward, and tolerate only fully formed adults. Tell the truth about performance. Make clear to managers that their top priority is building great teams. Leaders should create the company culture, and talent managers should think like innovative businesspeople and not fall into the traditional HR mind-set.

Laura reacted well: She was sad to be leaving but recognized that the generous severance would let her regroup, retrain, and find a new career path. This incident helped us create the other vital element of our talent management philosophy: If we wanted only "A" players on our team, we had to be willing to let go of people whose skills no longer fit, no matter how valuable their contributions had once been. Out of fairness to such people—and, frankly, to help us overcome our discomfort with discharging them—we learned to offer rich severance packages.

With these two overarching principles in mind, we shaped our approach to talent using the five tenets below.

Hire, Reward, and Tolerate Only Fully Formed Adults

Over the years we learned that if we asked people to rely on logic and common sense instead of on formal policies, most of the time we would get better results, and at lower cost. If you're careful to hire people who will put the company's interests first, who understand and support the desire for a high-performance workplace, 97% of your employees will do the right thing. Most companies spend endless time and money writing and enforcing HR policies to deal with problems the other 3% might cause. Instead, we tried really hard to not hire those people, and we let them go if it turned out we'd made a hiring mistake.

Adultlike behavior means talking openly about issues with your boss, your colleagues, and your subordinates. It means recognizing that even in companies with reams of HR policies, those policies are frequently skirted as managers and their reports work out what makes sense on a case-by-case basis.

Let me offer two examples.

When Netflix launched, we had a standard paid-time-off policy: People got 10 vacation days, 10 holidays, and a few sick days. We used an honor system—employees kept track of the days they took off and let their managers know when they'd be out. After we went public, our auditors freaked. They said Sarbanes-Oxley mandated that we account for time off. We considered instituting a formal tracking system. But then Reed asked, "Are companies *required* to give time off? If not, can't we just handle it informally and skip the accounting rigmarole?" I did some research and found that, indeed, no California law governed vacation time.

So instead of shifting to a formal system, we went in the opposite direction: Salaried employees were told to take whatever time they felt was appropriate. Bosses and employees were asked to work it out with one another. (Hourly workers in call centers and warehouses were given a more structured policy.) We did provide some guidance. If you worked in accounting or finance, you shouldn't plan to be out during the beginning or the end of a quarter, because those were busy times. If you wanted 30 days off in a row, you needed to meet with HR. Senior leaders were urged to take vacations and to let people know about them—they were role models for the policy. (Most were happy to comply.) Some people worried about whether the system would be inconsistent—whether some bosses would allow tons of time off while others would be stingy. In general, I worried more about fairness than consistency, because the reality is that in any organization, the highest-performing and most valuable employees get more leeway.

We also departed from a formal travel and expense policy and decided to simply require adultlike behavior there, too. The company's expense policy is five words long: "Act in Netflix's best interests." In talking that through with employees, we said we expected them to spend company money frugally, as if it were their own. Eliminating a formal policy and forgoing expense account police shifted responsibility to frontline managers, where it belongs. It also reduced costs: Many large companies still use travel agents (and pay their fees) to book trips, as a way to enforce travel policies. They could save money by letting employees book their own trips online. Like most Netflix managers, I had to have conversations periodically with employees who ate at lavish restaurants (meals that would have been fine for sales or recruiting, but not for eating alone or with a Netflix colleague). We kept an eye on our IT guys, who were prone to buying a lot of gadgets. But overall we found that expense accounts are another area where if you create a clear expectation of responsible behavior, most employees will comply.

Tell the Truth About Performance

Many years ago we eliminated formal reviews. We had held them for a while but came to realize they didn't make sense—they were too ritualistic and too infrequent. So we asked managers and employees to have conversations about performance as an organic part of their work. In many functions—sales, engineering, product development—it's fairly obvious how well people are doing. (As companies develop better analytics to measure performance, this becomes even truer.) Building a bureaucracy and elaborate rituals around measuring performance usually doesn't improve it.

Traditional corporate performance reviews are driven largely by fear of litigation. The theory is that if you want to get rid of someone, you need a paper trail documenting a history of poor achievement. At many companies, low performers are placed on "Performance Improvement Plans." I detest PIPs. I think they're fundamentally dishonest: They never accomplish what their name implies.

One Netflix manager requested a PIP for a quality assurance engineer named Maria, who had been hired to help develop our streaming service. The technology was new, and it was evolving very quickly. Maria's job was to find bugs. She was fast, intuitive, and hardworking. But in time we figured out how to automate the QA tests. Maria didn't like automation and wasn't particularly good at it. Her new boss (brought in to create a world-class automation tools team) told me he wanted to start a PIP with her.

I replied, "Why bother? We know how this will play out. You'll write up objectives and deliverables for her to achieve, which she can't, because she lacks the skills. Every Wednesday you'll take time away from your real work to discuss (and document) her shortcomings. You won't sleep on Tuesday nights, because you'll know it will be an awful meeting, and the same will be true for her. After a few weeks there will be tears. This will go on for three months. The entire team will know. And at the end you'll fire her. None of this will make any sense to her, because for five years she's been consistently rewarded for being great at her job—a job that basically doesn't exist anymore. Tell me again how Netflix benefits?

"Instead, let's just tell the truth: Technology has changed, the company has changed, and Maria's skills no longer apply. This won't be a surprise to her: She's been in the trenches, watching the work around her shift. Give her a great severance package—which, when she signs the documents, will dramatically reduce (if not eliminate) the chance of a lawsuit." In my experience, people can handle anything as long as they're told the truth—and this proved to be the case with Maria.

When we stopped doing formal performance reviews, we instituted informal 360-degree reviews. We kept them fairly simple: People were asked to identify things that colleagues should stop, start, or continue. In the beginning we used an anonymous software system, but over time we shifted to signed feedback, and many teams held their 360s face-to-face.

HR people can't believe that a company the size of Netflix doesn't hold annual reviews. "Are you making this up just to upset us?" they ask. I'm not. If you talk simply and honestly about performance on a regular basis, you can get good results—probably better ones than a company that grades everyone on a five-point scale.

Crafting a Culture of Excellence

NETFLIX FOUNDER AND CEO Reed Hastings discusses the company's unconventional HR practices.

HBR: Why did you write the Netflix culture deck?

Hastings: It's our version of *Letters to a Young Poet* for budding entrepreneurs. It's what we wish we had understood when we started. More than 100 people at Netflix have made major contributions to the deck, and we have more improvements coming.

Many of the ideas in it seem like common sense, but they go against traditional HR practices. Why aren't companies more innovative when it comes to talent management?

As a society, we've had hundreds of years to work on managing industrial firms, so a lot of accepted HR practices are centered in that experience. We're just beginning to learn how to run creative firms, which is quite different. Industrial firms thrive on reducing variation (manufacturing errors); creative firms thrive on *increasing* variation (innovation).

What reactions have you gotten from your peers to steps such as abolishing formal vacation and performance review policies? In general, do you think other companies admire your HR innovations or look askance at them?

My peers are mostly in the creative sector, and many of the ideas in our culture deck came from them. We are all learning from one another.

Which idea in the culture deck was the hardest sell with employees?

"Adequate performance gets a generous severance package." It's a pretty blunt statement of our hunger for excellence.

Have any of your talent management innovations been total flops?

Not so far.

Patty talks about how leaders should model appropriate behaviors to help people adapt to an environment with fewer formal controls. With that in mind, how many days off did you take in 2013?

"Days off" is a very industrial concept, like being "at the office." I find Netflix fun to think about, so there are probably no 24-hour periods when I never think about work. But I did take three or four weeklong family trips over the past year, which were both stimulating and relaxing.

Managers Own the Job of Creating Great Teams

Discussing the military's performance during the Iraq War, Donald Rumsfeld, the former defense secretary, once famously said, "You go to war with the army you have, not the army you might want or wish to have at a later time." When I talk to managers about creating great teams, I tell them to approach the process in exactly the opposite way.

In my consulting work, I ask managers to imagine a documentary about what their team is accomplishing six months from now. What specific results do they see? How is the work different from what the team is doing today? Next I ask them to think about the skills needed to make the images in the movie become reality. Nowhere in the early stages of the process do I advise them to think about the team they actually have. Only after they've done the work of envisioning the ideal outcome and the skill set necessary to achieve it should they analyze how well their existing team matches what they need.

If you're in a fast-changing business environment, you're probably looking at a lot of mismatches. In that case, you need to have honest conversations about letting some team members find a place where their skills are a better fit. You also need to recruit people with the right skills.

We faced the latter challenge at Netflix in a fairly dramatic way as we began to shift from DVDs by mail to a streaming service. We had to store massive volumes of files in the cloud and figure out how huge numbers of people could reliably access them. (By some estimates, up to a third of peak residential internet traffic in the U.S. comes from customers streaming Netflix movies.) So we needed to find people deeply experienced with cloud services who worked for companies that operate on a giant scale—companies like Amazon, eBay, Google, and Facebook, which aren't the easiest places to hire someone away from.

Our compensation philosophy helped a lot. Most of its principles stem from ideals described earlier: Be honest, and treat people like adults. For instance, during my tenure Netflix didn't pay performance bonuses, because we believed that they're unnecessary if you hire the right people. If your employees are fully formed adults who put the company first, an annual bonus won't make them work harder or smarter. We also believed in market-based pay and would tell employees that it was smart to interview with competitors when they had the chance, in order to get a good sense of the market rate for their talent. Many HR people dislike it when employees talk to recruiters, but I always told employees to take the call, ask how much, and send me the number—it's valuable information.

In addition, we used equity compensation much differently from the way most companies do. Instead of larding stock options on top of a competitive salary, we let employees choose how much (if any) of their compensation would be in the form of equity. If employees wanted stock options, we reduced their salaries accordingly. We believed that they were sophisticated enough to understand the trade-offs, judge their personal tolerance for risk, and decide what was best for them and their families. We distributed options every month, at a slight discount from the market price. We had no vesting period—the options could be cashed in immediately. Most tech companies have a four-year vesting schedule and try to use options as "golden handcuffs" to aid retention, but we never thought that made sense. If you see a better opportunity elsewhere, you should be allowed to take what you've earned and leave. If you no longer want to work with us, we don't want to hold you hostage.

We continually told managers that building a great team was their most important task. We didn't measure them on whether they were excellent coaches or mentors or got their paperwork done on time. Great teams accomplish great work, and recruiting the right team was the top priority.

Leaders Own the Job of Creating the Company Culture

After I left Netflix and began consulting, I visited a hot start-up in San Francisco. It had 60 employees in an open loft-style office with a foosball table, two pool tables, and a kitchen, where a chef cooked lunch for the entire staff. As the CEO showed me around, he talked about creating a fun atmosphere. At one point I asked him what the most important value for his company was. He replied, "Efficiency."

"OK," I said. "Imagine that I work here, and it's 2:58 p.m. I'm playing an intense game of pool, and I'm winning. I estimate that I can finish the game in five minutes. We have a meeting at 3:00. Should I stay and win the game or cut it short for the meeting?"

"You should finish the game," he insisted. I wasn't surprised; like many tech start-ups, this was a casual place, where employees wore hoodies and brought pets to work, and that kind of casualness often extends to punctuality. "Wait a second," I said. "You told me that efficiency is your most important cultural value. It's not efficient to delay a meeting and keep coworkers waiting because of a pool game. Isn't there a mismatch between the values you're talking up and the behaviors you're modeling and encouraging?"

When I advise leaders about molding a corporate culture, I tend to see three issues that need attention. This type of mismatch is one. It's a particular problem at start-ups, where there's a premium on casualness that can run counter to the high-performance ethos leaders want to create. I often sit in on company meetings to get a sense of how people operate. I frequently see CEOs who are clearly winging it. They lack a real agenda. They're working from slides that were obviously put together an hour before or were recycled from the previous round of VC meetings. Workers notice these things, and if they see a leader who's not fully prepared and who relies on charm, IQ, and improvisation, it affects how they perform, too. It's a waste of time to articulate ideas about values and culture if you don't model and reward behavior that aligns with those goals.

The second issue has to do with making sure employees understand the levers that drive the business. I recently visited a Texas start-up whose employees were mostly engineers in their twenties. "I bet half the people in this room have never read a P&L," I said to the CFO. He replied, "It's true—they're not financially savvy or business savvy, and our biggest challenge is teaching them how the business works." Even if you've hired people who want to perform well, you need to clearly communicate how the company makes money and what behaviors will drive its success. At Netflix, for instance, employees used to focus too heavily on subscriber growth, without much awareness that our expenses often ran ahead of it: We were spending huge amounts buying DVDs, setting up distribution centers, and ordering original programming, all before we'd collected a cent from our new subscribers. Our employees needed to learn that even though revenue was growing, managing expenses really mattered.

The third issue is something I call the split personality start-up. At tech companies this usually manifests itself as a schism between the engineers and the sales team, but it can take other forms. At Netflix, for instance, I sometimes had to remind people that there were big differences between the salaried professional staff at headquarters and the hourly workers in the call centers. At one point our finance team wanted to shift the whole company to direct-deposit paychecks, and I had to point out that some of our hourly workers didn't have bank accounts. That's a small example, but it speaks to a larger point: As leaders build a company culture, they need to be aware of subcultures that might require different management.

Good Talent Managers Think Like Businesspeople and Innovators First, and Like HR People Last

Throughout most of my career I've belonged to professional associations of human resources executives. Although I like the people in these groups personally, I often find myself disagreeing with them. Too many devote time to morale improvement initiatives. At some places entire teams focus on getting their firm onto lists of "Best Places to Work" (which, when you dig into the methodologies, are really based just on perks and benefits). At a recent conference I met someone from a company that had appointed a "chief happiness officer"—a concept that makes me slightly sick.

During 30 years in business I've never seen an HR initiative that improved morale. HR departments might throw parties and hand out T-shirts, but if the stock price is falling or the company's products aren't perceived as successful, the people at those parties will quietly complain—and they'll use the T-shirts to wash their cars.

Instead of cheerleading, people in my profession should think of themselves as businesspeople. What's good for the company? How do we communicate that to employees? How can we help every worker understand what we mean by high performance?

Here's a simple test: If your company has a performance bonus plan, go up to a random employee and ask, "Do you know specifically what you should be doing right now to increase your bonus?" If he or she can't answer, the HR team isn't making things as clear as they need to be.

At Netflix I worked with colleagues who were changing the way people consume filmed entertainment, which is an incredibly innovative pursuit—yet when I started there, the expectation was that I would default to mimicking other companies' best practices (many of them antiquated), which is how almost everyone seems to approach HR. I rejected those constraints. There's no reason the HR team can't be innovative too.

Originally published in January–February 2014. Reprint R1401E

Blue Ocean
Leadership

by W. Chan Kim and Renée Mauborgne

IT'S A SAD TRUTH ABOUT THE WORKPLACE: Just **30%** of employees are actively committed to doing a good job. According to Gallup's 2013 *State of the American Workplace* report, **50%** of employees merely put their time in, while the remaining **20%** act out their discontent in counterproductive ways, negatively influencing their coworkers, missing days on the job, and driving customers away through poor service. Gallup estimates that the **20%** group alone costs the U.S. economy around half a trillion dollars each year.

What's the reason for the widespread employee disengagement? According to Gallup, poor leadership is a key cause.

Most executives—not just those in America—recognize that one of their biggest challenges is closing the vast gulf between the potential and the realized talent and energy of the people they lead. As one CEO put it, "We have a large workforce that has an appetite to do a good job up and down the ranks. If we can transform them—tap into them through effective leadership—there will be an awful lot of people out there doing an awful lot of good."

Of course, managers don't intend to be poor leaders. The problem is that they lack a clear understanding of just what changes it would take to bring out the best in everyone and achieve high impact. We believe that leaders can obtain this understanding through an approach we call "blue ocean leadership." It draws on our research on blue ocean strategy, our model for creating new market space by converting noncustomers into customers, and applies its concepts and analytic frameworks to help leaders release the blue ocean of unexploited talent and energy in their organizations—rapidly and at low cost.

The underlying insight is that leadership, in essence, can be thought of as a service that people in an organization "buy" or "don't buy." Every leader in that sense has customers: the bosses to whom the leader must deliver performance, and the followers who need the leader's guidance and support to achieve. When people value your leadership practices, they in effect buy your leadership. They're inspired to excel and act with commitment. But when employees don't buy your leadership, they disengage, becoming noncustomers of your leadership. Once we started thinking about leadership in this way, we began to see that the concepts and frameworks we were developing to create new demand by converting noncustomers into customers could be adapted to help leaders convert disengaged employees into engaged ones.

Over the past 10 years we and Gavin Fraser, a Blue Ocean Strategy Network expert, have interviewed hundreds of people in organizations to understand where leadership was falling short and how it could be transformed while conserving leaders' most precious resource: time. In this article we present the results of our research.

Key Differences from Conventional Leadership Approaches

Blue ocean leadership rapidly brings about a step change in leadership strength. It's distinct from traditional leadership development approaches in several overarching ways. Here are the three most salient:

Focus on acts and activities

Over many years a great deal of research has generated insights into the values, qualities, and behavioral styles that make for good leadership, and these have formed the basis of development programs

Idea in Brief

The Problem

According to Gallup, only 30% of employees actively apply their talent and energy to move their organizations forward. Fifty percent are just putting their time in, while the remaining 20% act out their discontent in counterproductive ways. Gallup estimates that the 20% group alone costs the U.S. economy around half a trillion dollars each year. A main cause of employee disengagement is poor leadership, Gallup says.

The Solution

A new approach called blue ocean leadership can release the sea of unexploited talent and energy in organizations. It involves a four-step process that allows leaders to gain a clear understanding of just what changes it would take to bring out the best in their people,

while conserving their most precious resource: time. An analytic tool, the Leadership Canvas, shows leaders what activities they need to eliminate, reduce, raise, and create to convert disengaged employees into engaged ones.

Case in Point

A British retail group applied blue ocean leadership to redefine what effectiveness meant for frontline, midlevel, and senior leaders. The impact was significant. On the front line, for example, employee turnover dropped from about 40% to 11% in the first year, reducing recruitment and training costs by 50%. Factoring in reduced absenteeism, the group saved more than $50 million in the first year, while customer satisfaction scores climbed by over 30%.

and executive coaching. The implicit assumption is that changes in values, qualities, and behavioral styles ultimately translate into high performance.

But when people look back on these programs, many struggle to find evidence of notable change. As one executive put it, "Without years of dedicated efforts, how can you transform a person's character or behavioral traits? And can you really measure and assess whether leaders are embracing and internalizing these personal traits and styles? In theory, yes, but in reality it's hard at best."

Blue ocean leadership, by contrast, focuses on *what acts and activities leaders need to undertake* to boost their teams' motivation and business results, not on *who leaders need to be*. This difference in emphasis is important. It is markedly easier to change people's acts and activities than their values, qualities, and behavioral traits. Of course, altering a leader's activities is not a complete solution, and having the right values, qualities, and behavioral traits matters. But activities are something that any individual can change, given the right feedback and guidance.

Connect closely to market realities

Traditional leadership development programs tend to be quite generic and are often detached from what firms stand for in the eyes of customers and from the market results people are expected to achieve. In contrast, under blue ocean leadership, the people who face market realities are asked for their direct input on how their leaders hold them back and what those leaders could do to help them best serve customers and other key stakeholders. And when people are engaged in defining the leadership practices that will enable them to thrive, and *those practices are connected to the market realities* against which they need to perform, they're highly motivated to create the best possible profile for leaders and to make the new solutions work. Their willing cooperation maximizes the acceptance of new profiles for leadership while minimizing implementation costs.

Distribute leadership across all management levels

Most leadership programs focus on executives and their potential for impact now and in the future. But the key to a successful organization is having empowered leaders at every level, because outstanding organizational performance often comes down to the motivation and actions of middle and frontline leaders, who are in closer contact with the market. As one senior executive put it, "The truth is that we, the top management, are not in the field to fully appreciate the middle and frontline actions. We need effective leaders at every level to maximize corporate performance."

Blue ocean leadership is designed to be applied across the three distinct management levels: *top, middle,* and *frontline*. It calls for profiles for leaders that are tailored to the very different tasks, degrees of power, and environments you find at each level. Extending leadership capabilities deep into the front line unleashes the latent talent and drive of a critical mass of employees, and creating strong distributed leadership significantly enhances performance across the organization.

The Four Steps of Blue Ocean Leadership

Now let's walk through how to put blue ocean leadership into practice. It involves four steps.

1. See your leadership reality

A common mistake organizations make is to discuss changes in leadership before resolving differences of opinion over what leaders are actually doing. Without a common understanding of where leadership stands and is falling short, a forceful case for change cannot be made.

Achieving this understanding is the objective of the first step. It takes the form of what we call as-is Leadership Canvases, analytic visuals that show just how managers at each level invest their time and effort, as perceived by the customers of their leadership. An organization begins the process by creating a canvas for each of its three management levels.

A team of 12 to 15 senior managers is typically selected to carry out this project. The people chosen should cut across functions and be recognized as good leaders in the company so that the team has immediate credibility. The team is then broken into three smaller subteams, each focused on one level and charged with interviewing its relevant leadership customers—both bosses and subordinates—and ensuring that a representative number of each are included.

The aim is to uncover how people experience current leadership and to start a companywide conversation about what leaders do and should do at each level. The customers of leaders are asked which acts and activities—good and bad—their leaders spend most of their time on, and which are key to motivation and performance but are neglected by their leaders. Getting at the specifics is important; the as-is canvases must be grounded in acts and activities that reflect each level's specific market reality and performance goals. This involves a certain amount of probing.

At a company we'll call British Retail Group (BRG), many interviewees commented that middle managers spent much of their time playing politics. The subteam focused on that level pushed for clarification and discovered that two acts principally accounted for this judgment. One was that the leaders tended to divide responsibility among people, which created uncertainty about accountability—and some internal competitiveness. The result was a lot of finger-pointing and the perception that the leaders were playing people against one another. The subteam also found that the leaders spent much of their time in meetings with senior management. This led subordinates to conclude that their leaders were more interested in maximizing political "face time" and spinning news than in being present to support them.

After four to six weeks of interviews, subteam members come together to create as-is Leadership Profiles by pooling their findings and determining, based on frequency of citation, the dominant leadership acts and activities at each level. To help the subteams focus on what really matters, we typically ask for no more than 10 to 15 leadership acts and activities per level. These get registered on the horizontal axis of the as-is canvas, and the extent to which leaders do them is registered on the vertical axis. The cap of 10 to 15 prevents the canvas from becoming a statement of everything and nothing.

The result is almost always eye-opening. It's not uncommon to find that 20% to 40% of the acts and activities of leaders at all three levels provide only questionable value to those above and below them. It's also not uncommon to find that leaders are underinvesting in 20% to 40% of the acts and activities that interviewees at their level cite as important.

At BRG, the canvas for senior managers revealed that their customers thought they spent most of their time on essentially middle-management acts and activities, while the canvas of middle managers indicated that they seemed to be absorbed in protecting bureaucratic procedures. Frontline leaders were seen to be focused on trying to keep their bosses happy by doing things like deferring customer queries to them, which satisfied their desire to be in control. When we asked team members to describe each canvas in a tagline, an exercise that's part of the process, they labeled the frontline Leadership Profile "Please the Boss," the middle-manager profile "Control and Play Safe," and the senior manager profile "Focus on the Day-to-Day." (For an example, see the exhibit "What middle managers actually do.")

The implications were depressing. The biggest "aha" for the subteams was that senior managers appeared to have scarcely any time to do the real job of top management—thinking, probing, identifying opportunities on the horizon, and gearing up the organization to capitalize on them. Faced with firsthand, repeated evidence of the shortcomings of leadership practices, the subteams could not defend the current Leadership Profiles. The canvases made a strong case for change at all three levels; it was clear that people throughout the organization wished for it.

2. Develop alternative Leadership Profiles

At this point the subteams are usually eager to explore what effective Leadership Profiles would look like at each level. To achieve this, they go back to their interviewees with two sets of questions.

The first set is aimed at pinpointing the extent to which each act and activity on the canvas is either a cold spot (absorbing leaders' time but adding little or no value) or a hot spot (energizing employees and inspiring them to apply their talents, but currently underinvested in by leaders or not addressed at all).

The second set prompts interviewees to think beyond the bounds of the company and focus on effective leadership acts they've observed outside the organization, in particular those that could have a strong impact if adopted by internal leaders at their level. Here fresh ideas emerge about what leaders could be doing but aren't. This is not, however, about benchmarking against corporate icons; employees' personal experiences are more likely to produce insights. Most of us have come across people in our lives who have had a disproportionately positive influence on us. It might be a sports coach, a schoolteacher, a scoutmaster, a grandparent, or a former boss.

What middle managers actually do

As-is Leadership Canvases show the activities that employees see leaders engaging in, and the amount of time and energy they think leaders spend on each. The canvas below, for middle managers at the retail company BRG, reveals that people viewed them as rule enforcers who played it safe.

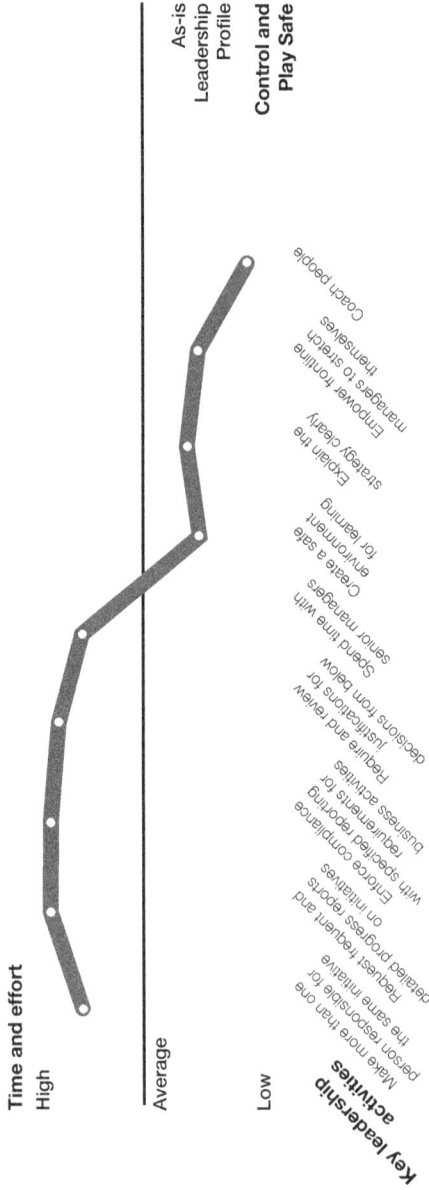

Time and effort

High

Average

Low

As-is Leadership Profile

Control and Play Safe

Key leadership activities

- Make more than one person responsible for the same initiative
- Request frequent and detailed progress reports on initiatives
- Enforce compliance with specified reporting requirements for business activities
- Require and review justifications for decisions from below
- Spend time with senior managers
- Create a safe environment for learning
- Explain the strategy clearly
- Empower frontline managers to stretch themselves
- Coach people

Whoever those role models are, it's important to get interviewees to detail which acts and activities they believe would add real value for them if undertaken by their current leaders.

To process the findings from the second round of interviews, the subteams apply an analytic tool we call the Blue Ocean Leadership Grid (see the exhibit by the same name). For each leadership level the interview results get incorporated into this grid. Typically, we start with the cold-spot acts and activities, which go into the Eliminate or Reduce quadrants depending on how negatively interviewees judge them. This energizes the subteams right away, because people immediately perceive the benefits of stopping leaders from

The Blue Ocean Leadership Grid

The Blue Ocean Leadership Grid is an analytic tool that challenges people to think about which acts and activities leaders should do less of because they hold people back, and which leaders should do more of because they inspire people to give their all. Current activities from the leaders' "as-is" profiles (which may add value or not), along with new activities that employees believe would add a lot of value if leaders started doing them, are assigned to the four categories in the grid. Organizations then use the grids to develop new profiles of effective leadership.

Eliminate What acts and activities do leaders invest their time and intelligence in that should be eliminated?	**Raise** What acts and activities do leaders invest their time and intelligence in that should be raised well above their current level?
Reduce What acts and activities do leaders invest their time and intelligence in that should be reduced well below their current level?	**Create** What acts and activities should leaders invest their time and intelligence in that they currently don't undertake?

doing things that add little or no value. Cutting back on those activities also gives leaders the time and space they need to raise their game. Without that breathing room, a step change in leadership strength would remain largely wishful thinking, given leaders' already full plates. From the cold spots we move to the hot spots, which go into the Raise quadrant if they involve current acts and activities or Create for those not currently performed at all by leaders.

With this input, the subteams draft two to four "to-be" canvases for each leadership level. These analytic visuals illustrate Leadership Profiles that can lift individual and organizational performance, and juxtapose them against the as-is leadership profiles. The subteams produce a range of leadership models, rather than stop at one set of possibilities, to thoroughly explore new leadership space.

3. Select to-be Leadership Profiles

After two to three weeks of drawing and redrawing their Leadership Canvases, the subteams present them at what we call a "leadership fair." Fair attendees include board members and top, middle, and frontline managers.

The event starts with members of the original senior team behind the effort describing the process and presenting the three as-is canvases. With those three visuals, the team establishes why change is necessary, confirms that comments from interviewees at all levels were taken into account, and sets the context against which the to-be Leadership Profiles can be understood and appreciated. Although the as-is canvases often present a sobering reality, as they did at BRG, the Leadership Profiles are shown and discussed only at the aggregate level. That makes individual leaders more open to change, because they feel that everyone is in the same boat.

With the stage set, the subteams present the to-be profiles, hanging their canvases on the walls so that the audience can easily see them. Typically, the subteam that focused on frontline leaders will go first. After the presentation, the attendees are each given three Post-it notes and told to put one next to their favorite Leadership Profile. And if they find that canvas especially compelling, they can put up to three Post-its on it.

After all the votes are in, the company's senior executives probe the attendees about why they voted as they did. The same process is then repeated for the two other leadership levels. (We find it easier to deal with each level separately and sequentially, and that doing so increases voters' recall of the discussion.)

After about four hours everyone in attendance has a clear picture of the current Leadership Profile of each level, the completed Blue Ocean Leadership Grids, and a selection of to-be Leadership Profiles that could create a significant change in leadership performance. Armed with this information and the votes and comments of attendees, the top managers convene outside the fair room and decide which to-be Leadership Profile to move forward on at each level. Then they return and explain their decisions to the fair's participants.

At BRG, more than 125 people voted on the profiles, and fair attendees greeted the three that were selected with enthusiasm. The tagline for frontline leaders' to-be profile was "Cut Through the Crap." (Sadly, this was later refined to "Cut Through to Serve Customers.") In this profile, frontline leaders did not defer the vast majority of customer queries to middle management and spent less time jumping through procedural hoops. Their time was directed to training frontline personnel to deliver on company promises on the spot, resolve customer problems, quickly help customers in distress, and make meaningful cross-sales—leadership acts and activities that fired up the frontline workers, were sure to excite customers, and would have a direct impact on the company's bottom line.

"Liberate, Coach, and Empower" was the tagline for middle management's to-be profile. Here leaders' time and attention shifted from controlling to supporting employees. This involved eliminating and reducing a range of oversight activities—such as requiring weekly reports on customer calls received and funds spent on office supplies—that sapped people's energy and kept frontline leaders at their desks. The profile also included new actions aimed at managing, disseminating, and integrating the knowledge of frontline leaders and their staff. In practical terms, this meant spending much more time providing face-to-face coaching and feedback.

To-be Leadership Canvas
Frontline managers: Serve customers, not the boss

Current activities of BRG's frontline leaders vs. the activities employees think they should be doing

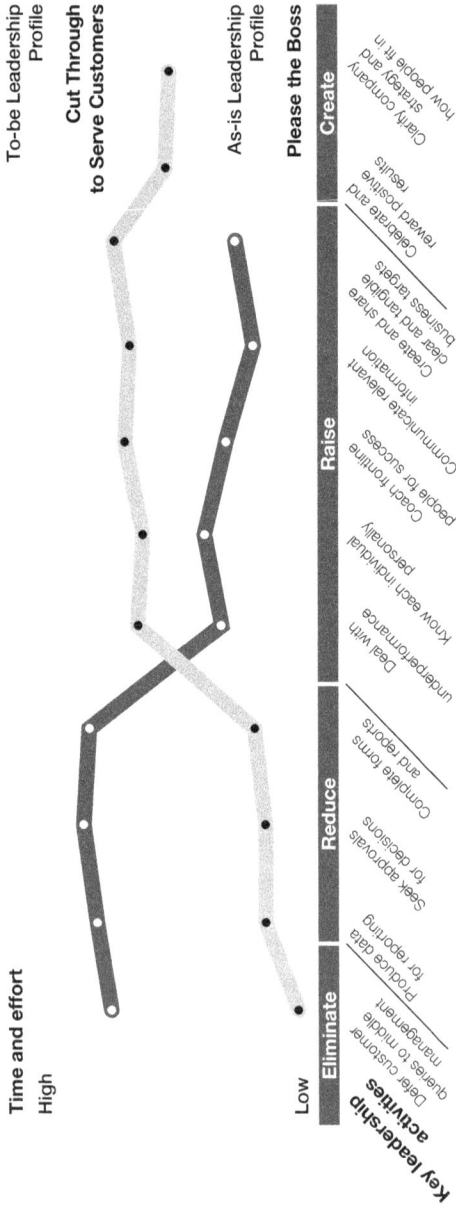

Time and effort

High

Low

To-be Leadership Profile

Cut Through to Serve Customers

As-is Leadership Profile

Please the Boss

Eliminate	Reduce		Raise					Create	

Key leadership activities

Defer customer queries to middle management

Produce data for reporting

Seek approvals for decisions

Complete forms and reports

Deal with underperformance

Know each individual personally

Coach frontline people for success

Communicate relevant information

Create and share clear and tangible business targets

Celebrate and reward positive results

Clarify company strategy and how people fit in

To-be Leadership Canvas
Middle Managers: More coaching, less control

Current activities of BRG's midlevel leaders vs. the activities employees think they should be doing

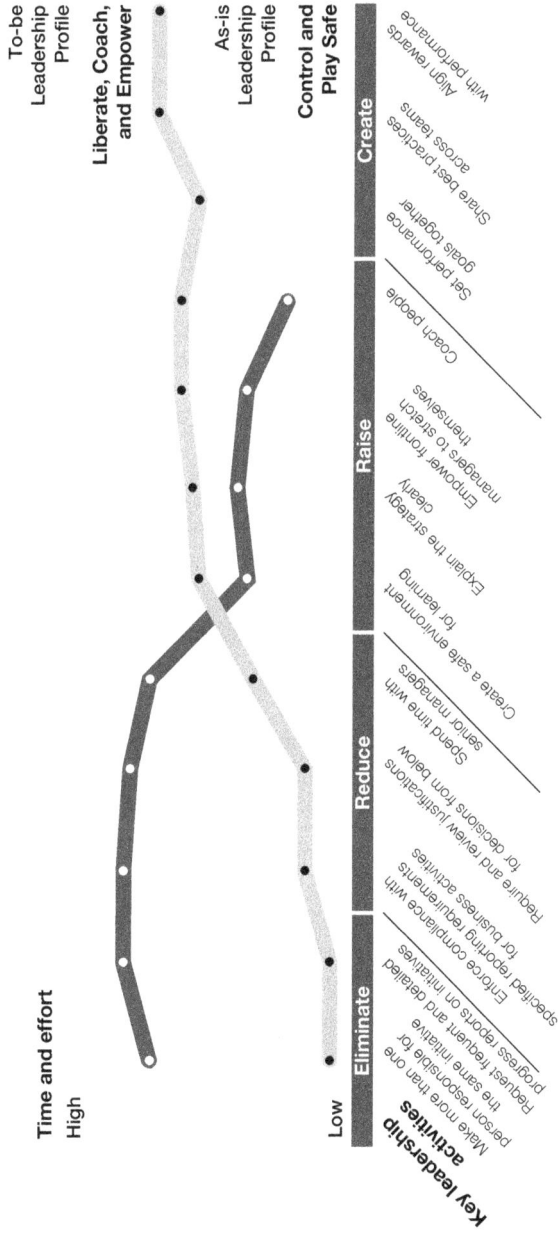

Time and effort
High

Low

To-be Leadership Profile

Liberate, Coach, and Empower

As-is Leadership Profile

Control and Play Safe

| Eliminate | Reduce | Raise | Create |

Key leadership activities

Make more than one person responsible for the same initiative

Request frequent and detailed progress reports on initiatives

Enforce compliance with specified reporting requirements for business activities

Require and review justifications for decisions from below

Spend time with senior managers

Create a safe environment for learning

Explain the strategy clearly

Empower frontline managers to stretch themselves

Coach people

Set performance goals together

Share best practices across teams

Align rewards with performance

The tagline for the to-be profile of senior management was "Delegate and Chart the Company's Future." With the acts and activities of frontline and middle managers reset, senior managers would be freed up to devote a significant portion of their time to thinking about the big picture—the changes in the industry and their implications for strategy and the organization. They would spend less time putting out fires.

The board members who attended the leadership fair felt strongly that the to-be Leadership Profiles supported the interests of customers as well as shareholders' profit and growth objectives. The frontline leaders were energized and ready to charge ahead. Senior managers went from feeling towed under the waves by all the middle-management duties they had to coordinate and attend to, to feeling as if they could finally get their heads above water and see the beauty of the ocean they had to chart.

The trickiest to-be Leadership Profile was middle management's. Letting go of control and empowering the people below them can be tough for folks in this organizational tier. But the to-be Leadership Profiles of both frontline and senior management helped clear the path to change at this level.

4. Institutionalize new leadership practices

After the fair is over, the original subteam members communicate the results to the people they interviewed who were not at the fair.

Organizations then distribute the agreed-on to-be profiles to the leaders at each level. The subteam members hold meetings with leaders to walk them through their canvases, explaining what should be eliminated, reduced, raised, and created. This step reinforces the buy-in that the initiative has been building by briefing leaders throughout the organization on key findings at each step of the process and tapping many of them for input. And because every leader is in effect the buyer of another level of leadership, all managers will be working to change, knowing that their bosses will be doing the same thing on the basis of input they directly provided.

The leaders are then charged with passing the message along to their direct reports and explaining to them how the new Leadership

To-be Leadership Canvas
Senior managers: From the day-to-day to the big picture

Current activities of BRG's senior managers vs. the activities employees think they should be doing

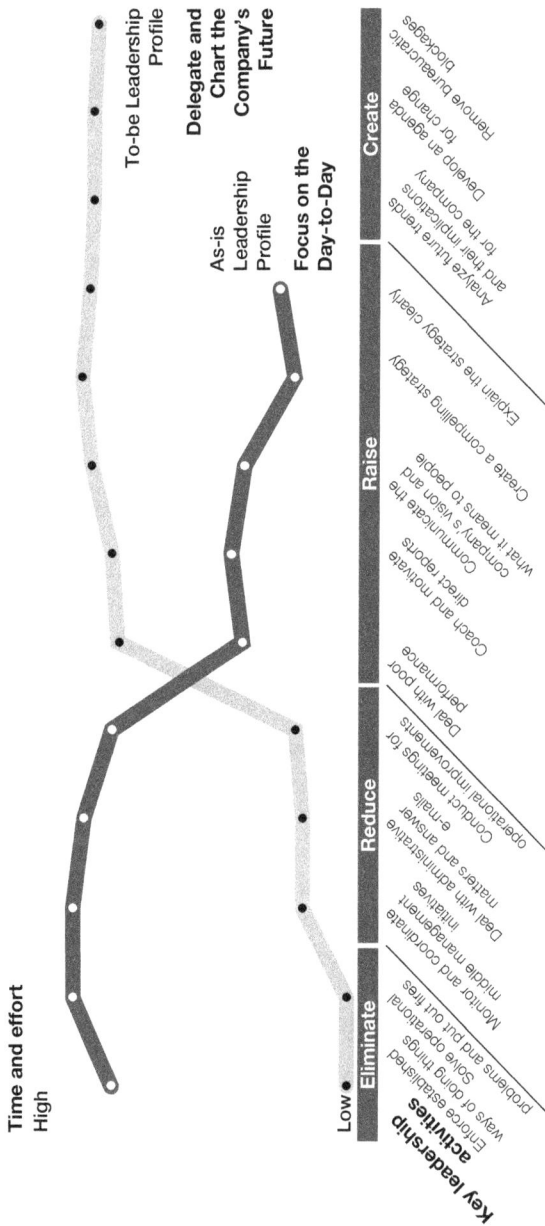

To-be Leadership Profile

Delegate and Chart the Company's Future

As-is Leadership Profile

Focus on the Day-to-Day

Time and effort

High

Low

Create
- Remove bureaucratic blockages
- Develop an agenda for change
- Analyze future trends and their implications for the company

Raise
- Explain the strategy clearly
- Create a compelling strategy
- Communicate the company's vision and what it means to people
- Coach and motivate direct reports

Reduce
- Deal with poor performance
- Conduct meetings for operational improvements
- Deal with administrative matters and answer e-mails

Eliminate
- Monitor and coordinate middle management initiatives
- Solve operational problems and put out fires
- Enforce established ways of doing things

Key leadership activities

Profiles will allow them to be more effective. To keep the new profiles top of mind, the to-be canvases are pinned up prominently in the offices of both the leaders and their reports. Leaders are tasked with holding regular monthly meetings at which they gather their direct reports' feedback on how well they're making the transition to the new profiles. All comments must be illustrated with specific examples. Has the leader cut back on the acts and activities that were to be eliminated and reduced in the new Leadership Profile? If yes, how? If not, in what instances was she still engaging in them? Likewise, is she focusing more on what does add value and doing the new activities in her profile? Though the meetings can be unnerving at first—both for employees who have to critique the boss and for the bosses whose actions are being exposed to scrutiny—it doesn't take long before a team spirit and mutual respect take hold, as all people see how the changes in leadership are positively influencing their performance.

Through the changes highlighted by the to-be profiles, BRG was able to deepen its leadership strength and achieve high impact at lower cost. Consider the results produced just at the frontline level: Turnover of BRG's 10,000-plus frontline employees dropped from about 40% to 11% in the first year, reducing both recruitment and training costs by some 50%. The total savings, including those from decreased absenteeism, amounted to more than $50 million that year. On top of that, BRG's customer satisfaction scores climbed by over 30%, and leaders at all levels reported feeling less stressed, more energized by their ability to act, and more confident that they were making a greater contribution to the company, customers, and their own personal development.

Execution Is Built into the Four Steps

Any change initiative faces skepticism. Think of it as the "bend over—here it comes again" syndrome. While blue ocean leadership also meets such a reaction initially, it counters it by building good execution into the process. The four steps are founded on the principles of fair process: engagement, explanation, and expectation clarity. The power of these principles cannot be overstated, and we have written extensively about their impact on the quality of execution for over 20 years. (See, for example, our article "Fair Process: Managing in the Knowledge Economy," HBR July–August 1997.)

In the leadership development context, the application of fair process achieves buy-in and ownership of the to-be Leadership Profiles and builds trust, preparing the ground for implementation. The principles are applied in a number of ways, with the most important practices being:

- **Respected senior managers spearhead the process.** Their engagement is not ceremonial; they conduct interviews and draw the canvases. This strongly signals the importance of the initiative, which makes people at all levels feel respected and gives senior managers a visceral sense of what actions are needed to create a step change in leadership performance. Here's a typical employee reaction: "At first, I thought this was just one of those initiatives where management loves to talk about the need for change but then essentially goes back to doing what they've always done. But when I saw that leading senior managers were driving the process and rolling up their sleeves to push the change, I thought to myself, 'Hmm . . . they may just finally mean it.'"

- **People are engaged in defining what leaders should do.** Since the to-be profiles are generated with the employees' own input, people have confidence in the changes made. The process also makes them feel more deeply engaged with their leaders, because they have greater ownership of what their leaders are doing. Here's what people told us: "Senior management said they were going to come and talk to people at all levels to understand what we need our leaders to do and not do, so we could thrive. And I thought, 'I'll believe it when someone comes knocking on my door.' And then they knocked."

- **People at all levels have a say in the final decision.** A slice of the organization across the three management levels gets to vote in selecting the new Leadership Profiles. Though the top managers have the final say on the to-be profiles and may not choose those with the most votes, they are required to provide a clear, sound explanation for their decisions in front of all attendees. Here's some typical feedback: "The doubts we had that our comments were just paid lip service to were dispelled when we saw how our inputs were figured into the to-be profiles. We realized then that our voices were heard."

- **It's easy to assess whether expectations are being met.** Clarity about what needs to change to move from the as-is to the to-be Leadership Profiles makes it simple to monitor progress. The monthly review meetings between leaders and their direct reports help the organization check whether it's making headway. We've found that those meetings keep leaders honest, motivate them to continue with change, and build confidence in both the process and the sincerity of the leaders. By collecting feedback from those meetings, top management can assess how rapidly leaders are making the shift from their as-is to their to-be Leadership Profiles, which becomes a key input in annual performance evaluations. This is what people say: "With the one-page visual of our old and new Leadership Profiles, we can easily track the progress in moving from the old to the new. In it, everyone can see with clarity precisely where we are in closing the gap."

Essentially, the gift that fair process confers is trust and, hence, voluntary cooperation, a quality vital to the leader-follower relationship. Anyone who has ever worked in an organization understands how important trust is. If you trust the process and the people you work for, you're willing to go the extra mile and give your best. If you don't trust them, you'll stick to the letter of the law that binds your contract with the organization and devote your energy to protecting your position and fighting over turf rather than to winning customers and creating value. Not only will your abilities be wasted, but they will often work against your organization's performance.

Becoming a Blue Ocean Leader

We never cease to be amazed by the talent and energy we see in the organizations we study. Sadly, we are equally amazed by how much of it is squandered by poor leadership. Blue ocean leadership can help put an end to that.

The Leadership Canvases give people a concrete, visual framework in which they can surface and discuss the improvements leaders need to make. The fairness of the process makes the implementation and monitoring of those changes far easier than in traditional top-down approaches. Moreover, blue ocean leadership achieves a transformation with less time and effort, because leaders are not trying to alter who they are and break the habits of a lifetime. They are simply changing the tasks they carry out. Better yet, one of the strengths of blue ocean leadership is its scalability. You don't have to wait for your company's top leadership to launch this process. Whatever management level you belong to, you can awaken the sleeping potential of your people by taking them through the four steps.

Are you ready to be a blue ocean leader?

Originally published in May 2014. Reprint R1405C

The Ultimate Marketing Machine

by Marc de Swaan Arons, Frank van den Driest, and Keith Weed

IN THE PAST DECADE, what marketers do to engage customers has changed almost beyond recognition. With the possible exception of information technology, we can't think of another discipline that has evolved so quickly. Tools and strategies that were cutting-edge just a few years ago are fast becoming obsolete, and new approaches are appearing every day.

Yet in most companies the organizational structure of the marketing function hasn't changed since the practice of brand management emerged, more than 40 years ago. Hidebound hierarchies from another era are still commonplace.

Marketers understand that their organizations need an overhaul, and many chief marketing officers are tearing up their org charts. But in our research and our work with hundreds of global marketing organizations, we've found that those CMOs are struggling with how to draw the new chart. What does the ideal structure look like? Our answer is that this is the wrong question. A simple blueprint does not exist.

Marketing leaders instead must ask, "What values and goals guide our brand strategy, what capabilities drive marketing excellence, and what structures and ways of working will support them?" Structure must follow strategy—not the other way around.

Former McDonald's CMO Larry Light understood that principle when he became the chief brand officer of the InterContinental Hotels Group, where the marketing team was intent on reorganizing its operation. Light quickly focused the team on defining marketing's purpose, its goals, and a process for achieving them. Once those had been clarified, a rational reorganization could occur.

To understand what separates the strategies and structures of superior marketing organizations from the rest, EffectiveBrands—in partnership with the Association of National Advertisers, the World Federation of Advertisers, Spencer Stuart, *Forbes,* MetrixLab, and Adobe—initiated Marketing2020, which to our knowledge is the most comprehensive marketing leadership study ever undertaken. Coauthor Keith Weed, the CMO of Unilever, is the chairman of the initiative's advisory board. To date the study has included in-depth qualitative interviews with more than 350 CEOs, CMOs, and agency heads, and over a dozen CMO roundtables in cities worldwide. We also conducted online quantitative surveys of 10,000-plus marketers from 92 countries. The surveys encompassed more than 80 questions focusing on marketers' data analytics capabilities, brand strategy, cross-functional and global interactions, and employee training.

We divided the survey respondents into two groups, overperformers and underperformers, on the basis of their companies' three-year revenue growth relative to their competitors'. We then compared those two groups' strategies, structures, and capabilities. Some of what we found should come as no surprise: Companies that are sophisticated in their use of data grow faster, for instance. Nevertheless, the research shed new light on the constellation of brand attributes required for superior marketing performance and on the nature of the organizations that achieve it. It's clear that "marketing" is no longer a discrete entity (and woe to the company whose marketing is still siloed) but now extends throughout the firm, tapping virtually every function. And while the titles, roles, and responsibilities of marketing leaders vary widely among companies and industries, the challenges they face—and what they must do to succeed—are deeply similar.

Idea in Brief

The Challenge

How marketers engage with customers has profoundly changed. Yet in most companies the organization of the marketing function is stuck in the past. What strategies, structures, and capabilities should marketers adopt to excel?

The Research

The Marketing2020 study surveyed more than 10,000 marketing executives globally about their organizations' data analytics capabilities, brand strategy, cross-functional and global interactions, employee engagement, and other factors and compared the responses of high-performing and low-performing organizations.

The Conclusion

High performers excelled in their ability to leverage customer insight, communicate a societal purpose, and deliver a rich customer experience. They also demonstrated superior cross-functional collaboration, strategic focus, organizational agility, and training. New, fluid organizational structures facilitate these capabilities.

Winning Characteristics

The framework that follows describes the broad traits of high-performing organizations, as well as specific drivers of organizational effectiveness. Let's look first at the shared principles of high performers' marketing approaches.

Big data, deep insights

Marketers today are awash in customer data, and most are finding narrow ways to use that information—to, say, improve the targeting of messages. Knowing what an individual consumer is doing where and when is now table stakes. High performers in our study are distinguished by their ability to integrate data on what consumers are doing with knowledge of *why* they're doing it, which yields new insights into consumers' needs and how to best meet them. These marketers understand consumers' basic drives—such as the desire to achieve, to find a partner, and to nurture a child—motivations we call "universal human truths."

The Nike+ suite of personal fitness products and services, for instance, combines a deep understanding of what makes athletes tick

---

Use of data distinguishes the leading brands

% of respondents who said that their organization leveraged all data and analytics to improve marketing effectiveness

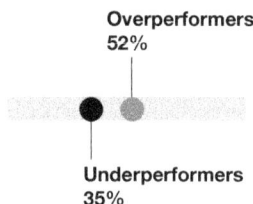

Overperformers
52%

Underperformers
35%

---

with troves of data. Nike+ incorporates sensor technologies embedded in running shoes and wearable devices that connect with the web, apps for tablets and smartphones, training programs, and social networks. In addition to tracking running routes and times, Nike+ provides motivational feedback and links users to communities of friends, like-minded athletes, and even coaches. Users receive personalized coaching programs that monitor their progress. An aspiring first-time half-marathon runner, say, and a seasoned runner rebounding from an injury will receive very different coaching. People are rewarded for good performance, can post their accomplishments on social media, and can compare their performance with—and learn from—others in the Nike+ community.

Purposeful positioning
Top brands excel at delivering all three manifestations of brand purpose—functional benefits, or the job the customer buys the brand to do (think of the pick-me-up Starbucks coffee provides); emotional benefits, or how it satisfies a customer's emotional needs (drinking coffee is a social occasion); and societal benefits, such as sustainability (when coffee is sourced through fair trade). Consider the Unilever Sustainable Living Plan, which defines a set of guiding principles for sustainable growth that emphasize improving health, reducing environmental impact, and enhancing livelihoods. The

---

Purpose-based positioning boosts sales

% of respondents who said that their organization's revenue growth was higher than competitors'

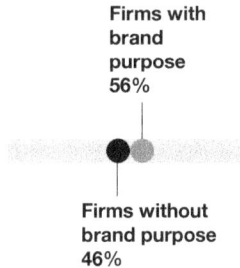

Firms with
brand
purpose
56%

Firms without
brand purpose
46%

---

plan lies at the heart of all Unilever's brand strategies, as well as its employee and operational strategies.

In addition to engaging customers and inspiring employees, a powerful and clear brand purpose improves alignment throughout the organization and ensures consistent messaging across touchpoints. AkzoNobel's Dulux, one of the world's leading paint brands, offers a case in point. In 2006, AkzoNobel was operating a heavily decentralized business structured around local markets, with each local business setting its own brand and business goals and developing its own marketing mix. Not surprisingly, the outcome was inconsistent brand positioning and results; Dulux soared in some markets and floundered in others. In 2008, Dulux's new global brand team pursued a sweeping program to understand how people perceived the brand across markets, paint's purpose in their lives, and the human truths that inspired people to color their environments. From China, to India, to the UK, to Brazil, a consistent theme emerged: The colors around us powerfully influence how we feel. Dulux wasn't selling cans of paint; it was selling "tins of optimism." This new definition of Dulux's brand purpose led to a marketing campaign, "Let's Color." It enlists volunteers, which now include more than 80% of AkzoNobel employees, and donates paint (more than half a million liters so far) to revitalize run-down urban neighborhoods, from the favelas of Rio to the streets of Jodhpur. In addition to aligning the once-decentralized marketing organization, Dulux's purpose-driven approach has expanded its share in many markets.

Total experience

Companies are increasingly enhancing the value of their products by creating customer experiences. Some deepen the customer relationship by leveraging what they know about a given customer to personalize offerings. Others focus on the breadth of the relationship by adding touchpoints. Our research shows that high-performing brands do both—providing what we call "total experience." In fact, we believe that the most important marketing metric will soon change from "share of wallet" or "share of voice" to "share of experience."

McCormick, the spices and flavorings firm, emphasizes both depth and breadth in delivering on its promise to "push the art, science, and passion of flavor." It creates a consistent experience for consumers across numerous physical and digital touchpoints, such as product packaging, branded content like cookbooks, retail stores, and even an interactive service, FlavorPrint, that learns each customer's taste preferences and makes tailored recipe recommendations. FlavorPrint does for recipes what Netflix has done for movies; its algorithm distills each recipe into a unique flavor profile, which can be matched to a consumer's taste-preference profile. FlavorPrint can then generate customized e-mails, shopping lists, and recipes optimized for tablets and mobile devices.

Organizing for Growth

Marketing has become too important to be left just to the marketers in a company. We say this not to disparage marketers but to underscore how holistic marketing now is. To deliver a seamless experience, one informed by data and imbued with brand purpose, all employees in the company, from store clerks and phone center reps to IT specialists and the marketing team itself, must share a common vision.

Our research has identified five drivers of organizational effectiveness. The leaders of high-performing companies connect marketing to the business strategy and to the rest of the organization; inspire their organizations by engaging all levels with the brand purpose; focus their people on a few key priorities; organize agile, cross-functional teams; and build the internal capabilities needed for success.

Connecting

In our work with marketing organizations, we have seen case after case of dysfunctional teamwork, suboptimal collaboration, and lack of shared purpose and trust.

Despite cultural and geographic obstacles, our high-performing marketers avoid such breakdowns for the most part. Their leaders excel at linking their departments to general management and other functions. They create a tight relationship with the CEO, making certain that marketing goals support company goals; bridge organizational silos by integrating marketing and other disciplines; and ensure that global, regional, and local marketing teams work interdependently.

Marketing historically has marched to its own drummer, at best unevenly supporting strategy handed down from headquarters and, more commonly, pursuing brand or marketing goals (such as

---

Connecting to corporate strategy

% of respondents who said that in their organization marketing is regarded as a strategic partner for business growth

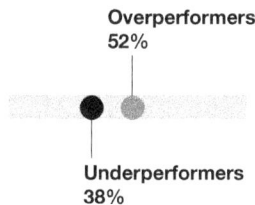

Overperformers
52%

Underperformers
38%

---

growing brand equity) that were not directly related to the overall business strategy. Today high-performing marketing leaders don't just align their department's activities with company strategy; they actively engage in creating it. From 2006 to 2013, our surveys show, marketing's influence on strategy development increased by 20 percentage points. And when marketing demonstrates that it is fighting for the same business objectives as its peers, trust and communication strengthen across all functions and, as we shall see, enable the collaboration required for high performance.

Another way companies foster connections is by putting marketing and other functions under a single leader. Motorola's Eduardo Conrado is the senior VP of both marketing and IT. A year after Antonio Lucio was appointed CMO of Visa, he was invited to also lead HR and tighten the alignment between the company's strategy and how employees were recruited, developed, retained, and rewarded. Coauthor Keith Weed leads communications and sustainability, as well as marketing, at Unilever. And Herschend Family Entertainment, owner of the Harlem Globetrotters and various theme parks, has recently expanded CMO Eric Lent's role to chief marketing and consumer technology officer.

Inspiring

Inspiration is one of the most underused drivers of effective marketing—and one of the most powerful. Our research shows that high-performing marketers are more likely to engage customers and employees with their brand purpose—and that employees in those organizations are more likely to express pride in the brand.

Inspiration strengthens commitment, of course, but when it's rooted in a respected brand purpose, all employees will be motivated by the same mission. This enhances collaboration and, as more and more employees come into contact with customers, also helps ensure consistent customer experiences. The payoff is that everyone in the company becomes a de facto member of the marketing team.

The key to inspiring the organization is to do internally what marketing does best externally: create irresistible messages and programs that get everyone on board. At Dulux, that involved handing

---

Inspiring workers to get results

% of respondents who said their company ensures that all employees are fully engaged with the brand purpose

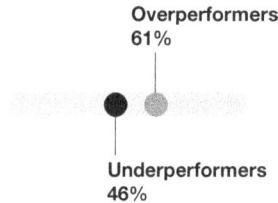

Overperformers
61%

Underperformers
46%

---

paint and brushes to thousands of employees and setting them loose on neighborhoods around the world. Unilever's leadership conducts a quarterly live broadcast with most of the company's 6,500 marketers to celebrate best brand practices and introduce new tools. In addition, Unilever holds a series of globally coordinated and locally delivered internal and external communications events, called Big Moments, to engage employees and opinion leaders companywide directly with the broader purpose of making sustainable living commonplace. Research shows this has led to a significant increase in employee commitment. Nike has a marketing staffer whose sole job is to tell the original Nike story to all new employees.

Inspiration is so important that many companies, Unilever among them, have begun measuring employees' brand engagement as a key performance indicator. Google does this by assessing employees' "Googliness" in performance appraisals to determine how fully people embrace the company's culture and purpose. And Zappos famously offers new hires $3,000 to leave after four weeks, effectively cutting loose anyone who is not inspired by the company's obsessive customer focus.

Focusing

When we asked eight global marketing executives in one organization to list their top five marketing objectives, only two goals made it onto everyone's list. The remainder was a motley assortment of personal or local objectives. Such misalignment, our data show, increases the farther teams are from an organization's center of power. With marketing activities ever more dispersed across global companies, that risk must be carefully managed.

By a wide margin, respondents in overperforming companies agreed with the statements "Local marketing understands the global strategy" and "Global marketing understands the local marketing reality." Winning companies were more likely to measure brands' success against key performance indicators such as revenue growth and profit and to tie incentives at the local level directly to those KPIs. Ironically, almost all companies were meticulous in planning and executing consumer communication campaigns but failed to devote the same care to internal communications about strategy. That's a dangerous oversight.

Marc Schroeder, the global marketing head for PepsiCo's Quaker brand, understood the need for internal cohesiveness when he led a cross-regional "marketing council" to develop and communicate the brand's first global growth strategy. The council defined a purposeful positioning, nailed down the brand's global objectives, set a prioritized growth agenda, created clear lines of accountability and incentives, and adopted a performance dashboard that tracked industry measures such as market share and revenue growth. The

---

Focusing on the right metrics

% of respondents who said that their brand's key performance indicators are clearly linked to overall business performance

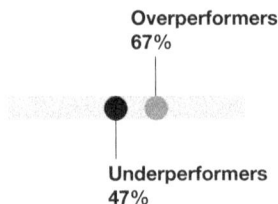

Overperformers
67%

Underperformers
47%

---

council communicated the strategy through regional and local team meetings, including those with agencies and retail customers worldwide, and hosted a first-ever global brand stewardship event to educate colleagues. As a result of those efforts, all Quaker marketing plans are now explicitly linked to one overall strategy.

Organizing for agility

Our research consistently shows that organizational structure, roles, and processes are among the toughest leadership challenges—and that the need for clarity about them is consistently underestimated or even ignored.

We have helped design dozens of marketing organizations. Typically we enter the scene after a traditional business consultancy has done preliminary strategy, cost, and head-count analyses, and our role is to work with the CMO to create and implement a new structure, operating model, and capability-building program. Though we believe there is no ideal organizational blueprint, our experience does suggest a set of operational and design principles that any organization can apply.

Today marketing organizations must leverage global scale but also be nimble, able to plan and execute in a matter of weeks or a few months—and, increasingly, instantaneously. Oreo famously took to Twitter during the blackout at the 2013 Super Bowl, reminding consumers, "You can still dunk in the dark," making the brand a trending topic during one of the world's biggest sporting events. That the tweet was designed and approved in minutes was no accident; Oreo deliberately organized and empowered its marketing team for the occasion, bringing agency and brand teams together in a "mission control" room and authorizing them to engage with their audience in real time.

Complex matrixed organizational structures—like those captured in traditional, rigid "Christmas tree" org charts—are giving way to networked organizations characterized by flexible roles, fluid responsibilities, and more-relaxed sign-off processes designed for speed. The new structures allow leaders to tap talent as needed from across the organization and assemble teams for specific, often short-term, marketing initiatives. The teams may form, execute, and disband in a matter of weeks or months, depending on the task.

New marketing roles. As companies expand internationally, they inevitably reorganize to better balance the benefits of global scale with the need for local relevance. Our research shows that, as a result, the vast majority of brands are led much more centrally today than they were a few years ago. Companies are removing middle, often regional, layers and creating specialized "centers of excellence" that guide strategy and share best practices while drawing on needed resources wherever, and at whatever level, they exist in the organization. As companies pursue this approach, roles and processes need to be adapted.

Marketing organizations traditionally have been populated by generalists, but particularly with the rise of social and digital marketing, a profusion of new specialist roles—such as digital privacy analysts and native-content editors—are emerging. We have found it useful to categorize marketing roles not by title (as the variety seems infinite) but as belonging to one of three broad types: "think" marketers, who apply analytic capabilities to tasks like data mining, media-mix modeling, and ROI optimization; "do" marketers, who develop content and design and lead production; and "feel" marketers, who focus on consumer interaction and engagement in roles from customer service to social media and online communities.

The networked organization. A broad array of skills and organizational tiers and functions are represented within each category. CMOs and other marketing executives such as chief experience officers and global brand managers increasingly operate as the orchestrators, assembling cross-functional teams from these three classes of talent to tackle initiatives. Orchestrators brief the teams, ensure that they have the capabilities and resources they need, and oversee performance tracking. To populate a team, the orchestrator and team leader draw from marketing and other functions as well as from outside agencies and consulting firms, balancing the mix of think, do, and feel capabilities in accordance with the team's mission. (See the exhibit "The orchestrator model.")

Companies are using this model to create task forces for a range of marketing programs, from integrating online and physical retail experiences to introducing new products. When Unilever launched Project Sunlight—a consumer-engagement program connected with its sustainable-living initiative—the team drew talent from seven expertise areas. The international cable company Liberty Global uses task forces to optimize the customer experience at key engagement points—such as when customers receive a bill. These teams are led by managers from a variety of marketing and nonmarketing functions, have different durations, and draw from each of the three talent pools in different measure.

The task-force model is both agile and disciplined. It requires a culture in which central leadership is confident that local teams understand the strategy and will collaborate to execute it. This works well only when everyone in the organization is inspired by the brand purpose and is clear about the goals. Google, Nike, Red Bull, and Amazon all embrace this philosophy. Amazon's Jeff Bezos captured the ethos when he said at a shareholders' meeting, "We are stubborn on vision. We are flexible on details."

Building capabilities

As we have shown, the most effective marketers lead by connecting, inspiring, focusing, and organizing for agility. But none of those activities can be fully accomplished, or sustained, without the continual building of capabilities. Our research shows pronounced differences in training between high- and low-performing companies, in terms of both quantity and quality.

At a minimum the marketing staff needs expertise in traditional marketing and communications functions—market research, competitive intelligence, media planning, and so forth. But we've seen that sometimes even those basic capabilities are lacking. Courses to onboard new staff and teach targeted skills are just the price of entry. The best marketing organizations, including those at Coca-Cola, Unilever, and the Japanese beauty company Shiseido, have invested

The orchestrator model

Drawing from a broad pool

CMOs and other marketing leaders such as chief experience officers and global brand leaders increasingly operate as orchestrators, tapping talent from both inside and outside the company to staff short-term task forces for specific initiatives.

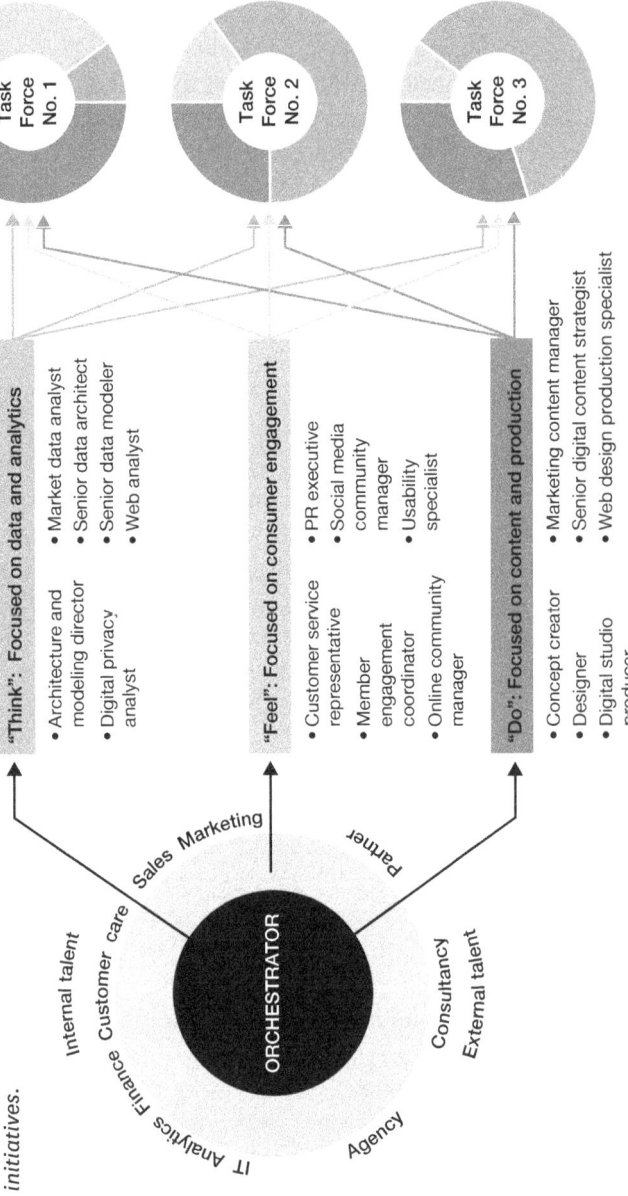

Creating teams with three key types of capabilities

The rise of social and digital media has changed the makeup of marketing teams, which were traditionally staffed by generalists. Today effective teams bring together people with three kinds of focus: "think," "feel," and "do."

Tailoring the team

The proportion of each type of capability on the team varies with its job.

"Think": Focused on data and analytics

- Architecture and modeling director
- Digital privacy analyst
- Market data analyst
- Senior data architect
- Senior data modeler
- Web analyst

"Feel": Focused on consumer engagement

- Customer service representative
- Member engagement coordinator
- Online community manager
- PR executive
- Social media community manager
- Usability specialist

"Do": Focused on content and production

- Concept creator
- Designer
- Digital studio producer
- Marketing content manager
- Senior digital content strategist
- Web design production specialist

ORCHESTRATOR

Internal talent
Customer care
Sales Marketing
Partner
IT Analytics Finance
Agency
Consultancy
External talent

Task Force No. 1

Task Force No. 2

Task Force No. 3

How Liberty Global applies the model

To improve customers' experience, the cable service provider Liberty Global set up task forces focused on individual touchpoints. Here's what some of the teams looked like and the results they got.

	Touchpoint	Key players	Team mix	Duration	Results
Task Force No. 1	Gets set-top box	**Leader:** Customer care executive **Functions involved:** IT, network, logistics, customer care, marketing	Thinkers 40% Feelers 10% Doers 50%	One year	**Problem:** Complex set-top box required too many on-site visits to set up. **Solution:** Developing remote installation guides and allowing remote installations by customer care agents.
Task Force No. 2	Receives first bill	**Leader:** Marketing executive **Functions involved:** Marketing, IT, customer care, billing	Thinkers 15% Feelers 60% Doers 25%	6 months	**Problem:** Customers found bills frustrating and confusing. **Solution:** Developing personalized video messages to explain the first bill.
Task Force No. 3	Sees new customer offer	**Leader:** Marketing executive **Functions involved:** R&D, IT, network, billing, marketing, customer care	Thinkers 10% Feelers 60% Doers 30%	3 months	**Problem:** Customer defections peaked when attractive offers were made to new customers. **Solution:** Extending the same offers to existing customers too, thus simplifying offerings.

Source: Visualization by Matt Perry

Building needed capabilities

% of respondents who said that their organization's training program was tailored to the specific needs of their business

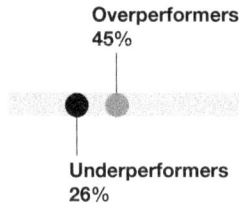

Overperformers
45%

Underperformers
26%

---

in dedicated internal marketing academies to create a single marketing language and way of doing marketing.

Senior managers across the company can benefit from programs for sharing expertise on consumer habits, competitor strategy, and retail dynamics. Virgin, Starbucks, and other corporations have created intensive "immersion" programs for this purpose. Executives at the director level can profit from advanced courses that focus on strategic considerations such as portfolio management and partnering. We find that senior leaders often gain a lot from digital and social media training, as they're frequently less well versed in those areas than their junior colleagues are. Appreciating this, companies including Unilever and Diageo have taken their senior leaders to Facebook for training. We've collaborated with partners at Google, MSN, and AOL to develop similar programs, including "reverse mentoring," which pairs very senior managers with younger staffers. Even the CMO can benefit from continued, targeted training. Visa's Antonio Lucio, for instance, hired a digital native to teach him about social media and monitor his progress.

Underperforming marketers, on the other hand, underinvest in training. Their employees receive just over half a day of training a year, on average, while overperformers give people nearly two full days of tailored, practical training by external experts.

At first blush, the Marketing2020 study reveals what you might expect: Marketers must leverage customer insight, imbue their brands with a brand purpose, and deliver a rich customer experience. They must connect, inspire, focus, organize, and build, as detailed here. The finding that's striking—and should serve as both a warning and a call to arms—is that most organizations haven't been able to put all those pieces together. Our data show that only half of even high-performing organizations excel on some of these capabilities. But that shouldn't be discouraging; rather, it illuminates where there's work to do. Regardless of how marketing delivers its messages in the future, the fundamental human motivations that marketers must satisfy won't change. The challenge now is to create organizations that can truly speak to those needs.

Originally published in July–August 2014. Reprint R1407C

Your Scarcest Resource

by Michael Mankins, Chris Brahm, and Gregory Caimi

MOST COMPANIES HAVE elaborate procedures for managing capital. They require a compelling business case for any new investment. They set hurdle rates. They delegate authority carefully, prescribing spending limits for each level.

An organization's *time,* in contrast, goes largely unmanaged. Although phone calls, e-mails, instant messages, meetings, and teleconferences eat up hours in every executive's day, companies have few rules to govern those interactions. In fact, most companies have no clear understanding of how their leaders and employees are spending their collective time. Not surprisingly, that time is often squandered—on long e-mail chains, needless conference calls, and countless unproductive meetings. This takes a heavy toll. Time devoted to internal meetings detracts from time spent with customers. Organizations become bloated, bureaucratic, and slow, and their financial performance suffers. Employees spend an ever-increasing number of hours away from their families and friends, with little to show for it.

Most advice about managing time focuses on individual actions. Coaches tell us to reassert control over our e-mail, be far more selective about which meetings we attend, and so on. Such recommendations are worthwhile, but executives often discover that their best intentions are overwhelmed by the demands and practices of their organizations. The e-mails and IMs keep coming. So do the meeting invitations. Ignore too many and you risk alienating your coworkers or your boss. And if this steady flood of interactions is how your company gets its work done, you have little choice in the matter: You have to plunge in and swim your way to the other side as best you can.

Some forward-thinking companies have taken a different approach entirely. They expect their leaders to treat time as a scarce resource and to invest it prudently. They bring as much discipline to their time budgets as to their capital budgets. These organizations have not only lowered their overhead expenses; they have liberated countless hours of previously unproductive time for executives and employees, fueling innovation and accelerating profitable growth.

By the Numbers: How Organizational Time Is Squandered

Andy Grove, the former CEO of Intel, once wrote, "Just as you would not permit a fellow employee to steal a piece of office equipment, you shouldn't let anyone walk away with the time of his fellow managers." Of course, such thievery happens often, unintentionally. Meetings creep onto the calendar with no clear plan or priority. Initiatives crop up, demanding management attention.

But companies now have time-management tools that weren't available in the past. With Microsoft Outlook, Google Calendar, iCal, and other scheduling and messaging applications, they can track where managers and employees are spending the organization's collective time and thus investing its resources. The calendar data show how many meetings are occurring each week, month, or year and what kind they are. They show how many people are attending, by level and function within the organization. They even permit the tracking of certain organizational behaviors, such as parallel processing and double booking, that occur before, during, and after meetings. Of course, a company scrutinizing such data needs strong safeguards to protect employee privacy; nobody wants the feeling that Big Brother is watching his every move. But this information can paint a vivid and revealing picture of an organization's time budget.

Bain & Company, using innovative people analytics tools from VoloMetrix (on whose board Chris Brahm sits), recently examined the time budgets of 17 large corporations. Here's what we discovered.

Companies are awash in e-communications

As the incremental cost of one-to-one and one-to-many communications has declined, the number of interactions has radically multiplied. Many executives now receive some 200 e-mails a day—more than 30,000 a year—and the increasing use of IM and crowdsourcing applications promises to compound the problem. (See the exhibit "The dark side of Metcalfe's Law.") If the trend is left unchecked, executives will soon be spending more than one day out of every week just managing electronic communications.

Meeting time has skyrocketed

Executives are also attending more meetings. That's partly because the cost of organizing them has dropped and partly because it's far easier than in the past for attendees to take part via telephone, videoconferencing, screen sharing, and the like. On average, senior executives devote more than two days every week to meetings involving three or more coworkers, and 15% of an organization's collective time is spent in meetings—a percentage that has increased every year since 2008. These gatherings proliferate. (See the exhibit "Ripple effects.")

Real collaboration is limited

Although the number of one-to-one and one-to-many interactions has risen dramatically over the past two decades, up to 80% of the interactions we reviewed took place within departments, not between businesses, across functions, or between headquarters and other parts of the company. As for the interactions that did extend beyond an individual unit, analysis of their content suggests that many of them involved the wrong people or took place for the wrong reason—that is, they were primarily for sharing information rather

The dark side of Metcalfe's Law

Metcalfe's Law states that the value of a telecommunications network increases exponentially with its size. In the 1970s communications were largely limited to telephone calls, telexes, and telegrams; on average, executives had to deal with fewer than 1,000 of them a year from people other than coworkers. That number rose dramatically as new technologies spread: We estimate that executives today receive an average of 30,000 external communications every year. And the more senior an executive, the more time subordinates must spend filtering, organizing, and coping with all those messages and conversations.

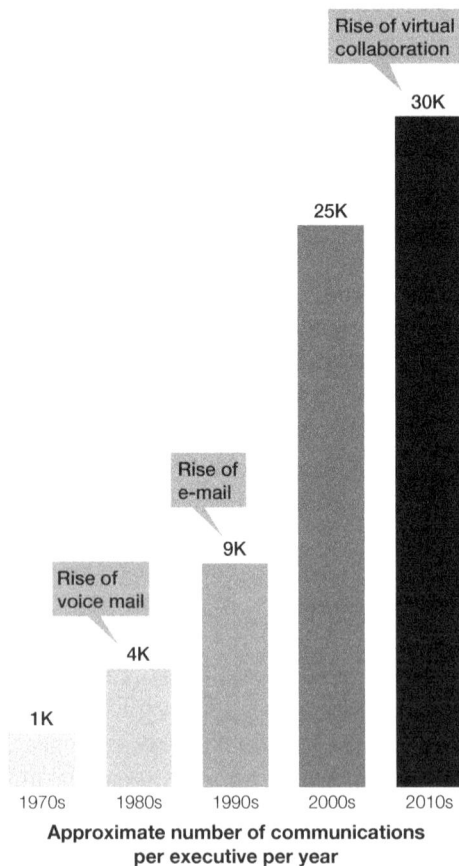

Rise of virtual collaboration

30K

25K

Rise of e-mail

9K

Rise of voice mail

4K

1K

| 1970s | 1980s | 1990s | 2000s | 2010s |

Approximate number of communications per executive per year

Idea in Brief

The Problem

Executives often discover that their best time-management intentions are overwhelmed by the demands and practices of the organization.

The Solution

Some companies have taken a new approach. They treat time as a scarce resource and bring as much discipline to their time budgets as to their capital budgets.

The Details

The new approach follows eight practices:

- Setting selective agendas

- Using a zero-based time budget

- Requiring a business case for each initiative

- Simplifying the organization

- Delegating authority for time investments

- Standardizing the decision process

- Making time discipline organization-wide

- Using feedback to manage organizational load

These practices enable companies to curb time pressure on executives, lower costs, and boost productivity.

than gathering input or brainstorming alternatives. In short, more time spent interacting has not produced significantly more collaboration outside organizational silos.

Dysfunctional meeting behavior is on the rise

At most of the organizations we examined, participants routinely sent e-mails during meetings. At one company, in 22% of meetings participants sent three or more e-mails, on average, for every 30 minutes of meeting time. Furthermore, executives commonly double-booked meetings and decided later which one they would actually attend. Dysfunctional behaviors like these create a vicious circle: Parallel processing and double booking limit the effectiveness of meeting time, so the organization sets up more meetings to get the work done. Those meetings prompt more dysfunctional behavior, and on and on.

Ripple effects

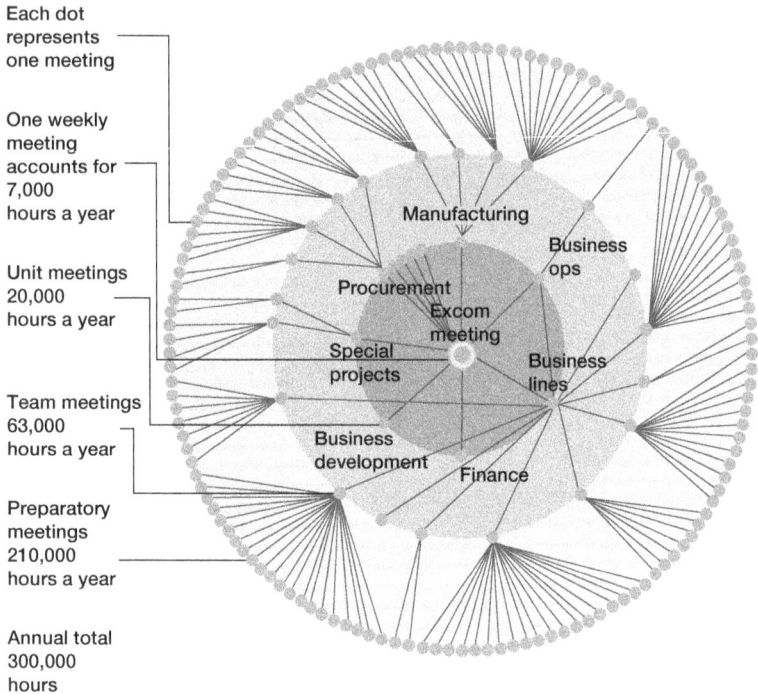

Each dot
represents
one meeting

One weekly
meeting
accounts for
7,000
hours a year

Unit meetings
20,000
hours a year

Team meetings
63,000
hours a year

Preparatory
meetings
210,000
hours a year

Annual total
300,000
hours

Manufacturing

Business
ops

Procurement

Excom
meeting

Special
projects

Business
lines

Business
development

Finance

The true cost of an excom meeting

*A single meeting at the top can consume significant organizational time and
money. At one company we worked with recently, the senior leadership team
reviewed performance across the business in weekly meetings that directly
consumed 7,000 person hours a year. In anticipation of those meetings, each
excom member met with his or her unit—consuming an additional 20,000
hours a year. The units, in turn, looked to their teams to generate and cross-
check critical information, usually in meetings, which ate up another 63,000
hours a year.*

*Preparatory meetings consumed a further 210,000 hours, bringing the total
time accounted for by weekly excom meetings to 300,000 hours a year—
which doesn't even include data collection and related work time.*

Formal controls are rare

At most companies no real costs are associated with requesting co-workers' time. If you want a meeting, your assistant merely sends out a meeting request or finds and fills an opening in the team's calendar. If you identify a problem in need of fixing, you convene a task force to study it and, most likely, launch an initiative to address it. Such demands on the organization's time typically undergo no review and require no formal approval.

There are few consequences

In a recent Bain survey, senior executives rated more than half the meetings they attended as "ineffective" or "very ineffective." Yet few organizations have established mechanisms for assessing the productivity of individual gatherings, not to mention clear penalties for unproductive sessions or rewards for particularly valuable ones.

It's hard to know exactly how much of this squandered time could be rescued. But our data suggest that most companies have an opportunity to liberate at least 20% of their collective hours by bringing greater discipline to time management.

Eight Practices for Managing Organizational Time

A handful of companies have learned how to attack this problem directly. They create formal budgets to manage organizational time as the scarce resource it is. They purposefully curb demands on executive time. And they push their people to improve the productivity of meetings and other forms of collaboration. We find that the following eight practices pay big dividends.

Make the agenda clear and selective

One hallmark of great leaders is their ability to separate the urgent from the merely important. They know that everyone must share an understanding of which activities are critical to success. We advocate broadening that understanding to include time priorities. Not only should people be crystal clear about how to spend any extra time they may find in their day, but they should know what they can safely postpone or ignore.

Perhaps no other executive managed organizational time more effectively than the late Steve Jobs. Focus was a key to Apple's success. Each year Jobs took Apple's top 100 executives off-site for a planning retreat and pushed them to identify the company's leading 10 priorities for the coming year. Members of the group competed intensely to get their ideas on the short list. Then Jobs liked to take a marker and cross out the bottom seven. "We can only do three," he would announce. His gesture made it clear to everyone present what the company would and would not take on. Jobs cut through the noise and enabled Apple to invest the time of its top talent strategically, without dilution or waste. This dramatically accelerated the pace of innovation at the company and helped it become one of the largest in the world by market capitalization.

Create a zero-based time budget

Increasing workforce productivity requires that every organizational asset be carefully managed. Accordingly, many companies develop their operating and capital budgets from scratch each year, rather than taking the previous year's budget as a starting point. The best companies have zero-based time budgets as well. Their mindset is: We will invest no additional organizational time in meetings; we will "fund" all new meetings through "withdrawals" from our existing meeting "bank."

Take Ford Motor Company. When Alan Mulally became Ford's CEO, in 2006, he discovered that the company's most senior executives spent a lot of time in meetings. In fact, the top 35 executives assembled every month for what they called "meetings week"— five days devoted to discussing auto programs and reviewing performance. The direct and indirect costs of these sessions were significant—far more than the company could afford at the time.

In late 2006 Mulally asked his team to ruthlessly assess the efficiency and effectiveness of the company's regular meetings. It quickly eliminated all unnecessary ones and shortened those that were unduly long, which forced people to maximize output per minute of meeting time. The team also became much more selective about requests for new meetings. Although individual managers at Ford are not required to eliminate one meeting before another can be scheduled, the company's executives treat organizational time as fixed. The centerpiece of Ford's approach is a weekly session called the Business Plan Review (BPR), which has replaced meetings week. It brings together the company's most senior executives in a focused four- to five-hour session each week to set strategy and review performance. Content for the session is standardized, reducing the extensive prep time previously required. The implementation of the BPR liberated thousands of hours at Ford, enabling the company to lower overhead costs at a time when rivals were seeking a government bailout. It also improved the quality and pace of decision making at the company, accelerating Ford's turnaround.

Require business cases for all new projects

Companies often fall victim to "initiative creep," as seemingly sensible projects are added incrementally. Few if any of them are ever formally terminated. When Gary Goldberg became CEO at Newmont Mining, in March 2013, 87 initiatives were under way across the company, each demanding the time and attention of one or more members of Newmont's executive leadership team (ELT). Many of those initiatives, including efforts to improve mine safety or increase operational efficiency, were valuable. Others were more questionable in terms of Newmont's return on investment.

To gain control over initiative creep, Goldberg insisted that leaders develop formal business cases for all the company's ongoing and proposed projects. Before investing any time in one of them, the ELT had to review the case and approve the effort. Each case had to specify the precise economic benefit the initiative would deliver and also its total cost—including the time of executive leaders. Every initiative was required to have an executive sponsor, who was accountable for managing its progress and keeping it on budget.

These requirements had the desired effect. Many of the projects that had been under way when Goldberg took over were discontinued because no business cases were presented for them. Others were not approved. After less than three months, Newmont had scaled back the number of initiatives by a third and refocused its collective time on improving safety and operational efficiency.

Simplify the organization

The more management layers between the CEO and the frontline worker, the slower the information flows and decision making. All managers know this, even if many fail to act on their understanding.

What they often don't realize is that every additional supervisor adds costs well beyond his or her salary. Supervisors schedule meetings; those meetings require content that some people must generate and others must review; and each meeting typically spawns even more meetings. We have found that on average, adding a manager to an organization creates about 1.5 full-time-equivalent employees' worth of new work—that is, his own plus 50% of another employee's—and every additional senior vice president creates more than 2.6. The "caravan" of resources accompanying a manager or a senior executive, which may include an executive assistant or a chief of staff, adds further work and costs. (See the exhibit "The true cost of your next manager.") As the work piles up, time grows ever shorter.

Given the direct and indirect costs of most supervisors, one way to improve organizational efficiency is to simplify, starting at the top. In 2010 the University of California at Berkeley was facing tremendous financial pressure: The state legislature had cut $150 million from Berkeley's budget in response to a mounting deficit. To safeguard the funds needed to preserve the university's reputation for excellence in teaching, research, and access, the administration had to find ways to streamline its cost structure.

In the summer of that year, Robert Birgeneau, then the university's chancellor, launched what was known as Operational Excellence. The program's objective was to dramatically improve the efficiency and effectiveness of the HR, finance, IT, and general administrative support provided to Berkeley's 14 colleges and more than 100 departments. By standardizing and simplifying work by function and sharing management across those units, Operational Excellence removed hundreds of unnecessary supervisors and freed

---

The true cost of your next manager

Every individual manager gets e-mail and meeting support from subordinates whose time should be factored into his or her job. As managers move up the hierarchy, their need for support staff grows.

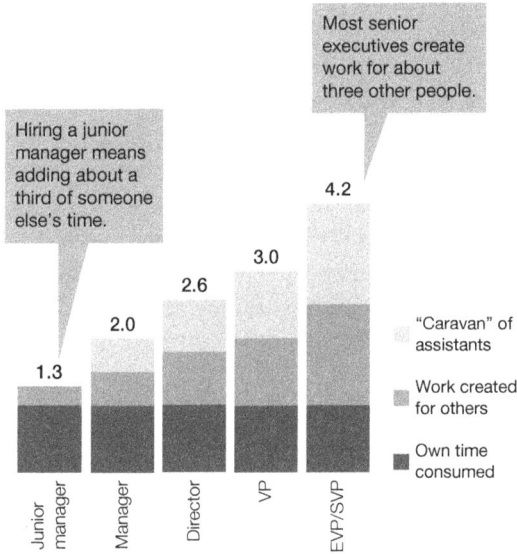

Most senior executives create work for about three other people.

Hiring a junior manager means adding about a third of someone else's time.

4.2

3.0

2.6

2.0

1.3

"Caravan" of assistants

Work created for others

Own time consumed

Junior manager | Manager | Director | VP | EVP/SVP

---

up an enormous amount of organizational time. The restructuring and simplification has saved the university some $120 million annually while enabling Berkeley to deliver more with less.

Clearly delegate authority for time investments

Most companies place few restrictions on who can organize a meeting. Decisions regarding how long the session should be, who should attend, and even whether participants must attend in person are frequently left up to low-level employees. The result: Costly meetings are scheduled without scrutiny.

For example, leaders at one large manufacturing company recently discovered that a regularly scheduled 90-minute meeting of midlevel managers cost more than $15 million annually. When asked "Who is responsible for approving this meeting?" the managers were at a loss. "No one," they replied. "Tom's assistant just schedules it and the team attends." In effect, a junior VP's administrative assistant was permitted to invest $15 million without supervisor approval. No such thing would ever happen with the company's financial capital.

At another manufacturing company we worked with recently, the leadership team took two simple steps to rein in unproductive meeting time. First, it reduced the default meeting length from 60 minutes to 30 minutes. Second, it established a guideline limiting meetings to seven or fewer participants. Any meeting exceeding 90 minutes or including more than seven people had to be approved by the supervisor of the convener's supervisor (two levels up). This cut the organizational time budget dramatically—by the equivalent of 200 full-time employees over a six-month period.

Standardize the decision process

At many companies, decision rights and processes are so ill defined that the organization devotes more time to managing the matrix than to decision making and execution. In such cases, establishing an organization-wide approach to decision making can greatly improve efficiency and rescue time for other purposes.

Woodside, Australia's largest independent oil and gas company, is illustrative. The company had been operating with a matrix structure for a number of years. Although the matrix was designed to foster greater collaboration across the company, decision authority and accountability were murky. As a result, the time spent coordinating across functions and business units was rising steeply, adding costs. In 2012 Woodside's leadership explicitly defined a set of operating principles that spelled out responsibilities, authority, and accountability for the business units, the functions, and the corporate center. A broad training program helped ensure that the company's top leaders understood the new principles and the implications for their units. A small network of navigators was established to help remove roadblocks and accelerate decision making across the company.

The impact of these changes has been profound. Given clarity on who is accountable for important decisions, executives at Woodside have streamlined how those decisions are made. A significant portion of the resulting saved time is now spent on efforts to improve execution and identify new growth opportunities.

Establish organization-wide time discipline

No company can eliminate all meetings—they are essential for fostering collaboration and making critical decisions. But most companies can dramatically improve the quality of the meetings they do hold by establishing a few simple norms:

- *Agendas with clear objectives.* At Intel all meetings start with a clear purpose: to inform about topic A, discuss topic B, and decide topic C. As simple as that may sound, the procedure focuses attendees on accomplishing the specified objectives.

- *Advance preparation.* At Ford, all materials for weekly Business Plan Reviews must be distributed in advance so that participants can review them before the meetings. That greatly reduces the time devoted to information sharing during BPRs.

- *On-time start.* Beginning each hour-long meeting only five minutes late costs a company 8% of its meeting time. Most management teams wouldn't tolerate 8% waste in any other area of responsibility.

- *Early ending, particularly if the meeting is going nowhere.* Steve Jobs used to "call an audible" when the productivity of a meeting at Apple started to decline or participants were unprepared. Some people considered his style abrupt, but he prevented the waste of time and money when sessions were unlikely to produce the desired outcome.

Provide feedback to manage organizational load

It's said that we can't manage what we don't measure. Yet few organizations routinely track the critical variables affecting human productivity, such as meeting time, meeting attendance, and e-mail volume. Without such monitoring, it is hard to manage those factors—or even to know the magnitude of your organization's productivity problem. And without a baseline measure of productivity, it is impossible to set targets for improvement.

Many executives already review how much time they spend with various constituencies and on various issues, using just their own calendars. A few companies, including Seagate and Boeing, are experimenting with giving their executives feedback on the "load" they are putting on the organization in terms of meetings, e-mails, IMs, and so forth. At Seagate some senior managers participated in a program in which they routinely received reports quantifying their individual loads along with the average load generated by other executives at their level and in their function. This information, combined with guidelines from the top, encouraged them to modify their behavior.

Time is an organization's scarcest—and most often squandered—resource. No amount of money can buy a 25-hour day or reclaim an hour lost in an unproductive meeting. To get the most out of your employees, you must treat their time as precious, creating disciplined time budgets and investing effort to generate the greatest possible value for your company.

Originally published in May 2014. Reprint R1405D

How Google Sold Its Engineers on Management

by David A. Garvin

SINCE THE EARLY DAYS OF GOOGLE, people throughout the company have questioned the value of managers. That skepticism stems from a highly technocratic culture. As one software engineer, Eric Flatt, puts it, "We are a company built by engineers for engineers." And most engineers, not just those at Google, want to spend their time designing and debugging, not communicating with bosses or supervising other workers' progress. In their hearts they've long believed that management is more destructive than beneficial, a distraction from "real work" and tangible, goal-directed tasks.

A few years into the company's life, founders Larry Page and Sergey Brin actually wondered whether Google needed any managers at all. In 2002 they experimented with a completely flat organization, eliminating engineering managers in an effort to break down barriers to rapid idea development and to replicate the collegial environment they'd enjoyed in graduate school. That experiment lasted only a few months: They relented when too many people went directly to Page with questions about expense reports, interpersonal conflicts, and other nitty-gritty issues. And as the company grew, the founders soon realized that managers contributed in many other, important ways—for instance, by communicating strategy, helping employees prioritize projects, facilitating collaboration, supporting career development, and ensuring that processes and systems aligned with company goals.

Google now has some layers but not as many as you might expect in an organization with more than 37,000 employees: just 5,000 managers, 1,000 directors, and 100 vice presidents. It's not uncommon to find engineering managers with 30 direct reports. Flatt says that's by design, to prevent micromanaging. "There is only so much you can meddle when you have 30 people on your team, so you have to focus on creating the best environment for engineers to make things happen," he notes. Google gives its rank and file room to make decisions and innovate. Along with that freedom comes a greater respect for technical expertise, skillful problem solving, and good ideas than for titles and formal authority. Given the overall indifference to pecking order, anyone making a case for change at the company needs to provide compelling logic and rich supporting data. Seldom do employees accept top-down directives without question.

Google downplays hierarchy and emphasizes the power of the individual in its recruitment efforts, as well, to achieve the right cultural fit. Using a rigorous, data-driven hiring process, the company goes to great lengths to attract young, ambitious self-starters and original thinkers. It screens candidates' résumés for markers that indicate potential to excel there—especially general cognitive ability. People who make that first cut are then carefully assessed for initiative, flexibility, collaborative spirit, evidence of being well-rounded, and other factors that make a candidate "Googley."

So here's the challenge Google faced: If your highly skilled, handpicked hires don't value management, how can you run the place effectively? How do you turn doubters into believers, persuading them to spend time managing others? As it turns out, by applying the same analytical rigor and tools that you used to hire them in the first place—and that they set such store by in their own work. You use data to test your assumptions about management's merits and then make your case.

Idea in Brief

The Challenge

Knowledge workers often doubt managers' contributions, especially in a technical environment. Until recently, that was the case at Google, a company filled with "A" players who considered management a distraction from the designing and debugging they loved to do.

The Solution

Google's people analytics team persuaded the skeptics with data. Applying the same rigor the company uses in hiring and operations, the team examined employee surveys, performance reviews, and double-blind interview responses to verify that management indeed mattered and to gather evidence of success.

The Outcome

People at Google now value management. The company has incorporated its findings into feedback reports, concrete guidelines, and hands-on training to help managers hone essential skills in eight key areas. Managers are improving as a result, and their direct reports are more satisfied.

Analyzing the Soft Stuff

To understand how Google set out to prove managers' worth, let's go back to 2006, when Page and Brin brought in Laszlo Bock to head up the human resources function—appropriately called people operations, or people ops. From the start, people ops managed performance reviews, which included annual 360-degree assessments. It also helped conduct and interpret the Googlegeist employee survey on career development goals, perks, benefits, and company culture. A year later, with that foundation in place, Bock hired Prasad Setty from Capital One to lead a people analytics group. He challenged Setty to approach HR with the same empirical discipline Google applied to its business operations.

Setty took him at his word, recruiting several PhDs with serious research chops. This new team was committed to leading organizational change. "I didn't want our group to be simply a reporting house," Setty recalls. "Organizations can get bogged down in all that data. Instead, I wanted us to be hypothesis-driven and help solve company problems and questions with data."

People analytics then pulled together a small team to tackle issues relating to employee well-being and productivity. In early 2009 it presented its initial set of research questions to Setty. One question stood out, because it had come up again and again since the company's founding: Do managers matter?

To find the answer, Google launched Project Oxygen, a multiyear research initiative. It has since grown into a comprehensive program that measures key management behaviors and cultivates them through communication and training. By November 2012, employees had widely adopted the program—and the company had shown statistically significant improvements in multiple areas of managerial effectiveness and performance.

Google is one of several companies that are applying analytics in new ways. Until recently, organizations used data-driven decision making mainly in product development, marketing, and pricing. But these days, Google, Procter & Gamble, Harrah's, and others take that same approach in addressing human resources needs. (See "Competing on Talent Analytics," by Thomas H. Davenport, Jeanne Harris, and Jeremy Shapiro, HBR October 2010.)

Unfortunately, scholars haven't done enough to help these organizations understand and improve day-to-day management practice. Compared with leadership, managing remains understudied and undertaught—largely because it's so difficult to describe, precisely and concretely, what managers actually do. We often say that they get things done through other people, yet we don't usually spell out how in any detail. Project Oxygen, in contrast, was designed to offer granular, hands-on guidance. It didn't just identify desirable management traits in the abstract; it pinpointed specific, measurable behaviors that brought those traits to life.

That's why Google employees let go of their skepticism and got with the program. Project Oxygen mirrored their decision-making criteria, respected their need for rigorous analysis, and made it a priority to measure impact. Data-driven cultures, Google discovered, respond well to data-driven change.

Making the Case

Project Oxygen colead Neal Patel recalls, "We knew the team had to be careful. Google has high standards of proof, even for what, at other places, might be considered obvious truths. Simple correlations weren't going to be enough. So we actually ended up trying to prove the opposite case—that managers don't matter. Luckily, we failed."

To begin, Patel and his team reviewed exit-interview data to see if employees cited management issues as a reason for leaving Google. Though they found some connections between turnover rates and low satisfaction with managers, those didn't apply to the company more broadly, given the low turnover rates overall. Nor did the findings prove that managers caused attrition.

As a next step, Patel examined Googlegeist ratings and semiannual reviews, comparing managers on both satisfaction and performance. For both dimensions, he looked at the highest and lowest scorers (the top and bottom quartiles).

"At first," he says, "the numbers were not encouraging. Even the low-scoring managers were doing pretty well. How could we find evidence that better management mattered when all managers seemed so similar?" The solution came from applying sophisticated multivariate statistical techniques, which showed that even "the smallest incremental increases in manager quality were quite powerful."

For example, in 2008, the high-scoring managers saw less turnover on their teams than the others did—and retention was related more strongly to manager quality than to seniority, performance, tenure, or promotions. The data also showed a tight connection between managers' quality and workers' happiness: Employees with high-scoring bosses consistently reported greater satisfaction in multiple areas, including innovation, work-life balance, and career development.

In light of this research, the Project Oxygen team concluded that managers indeed mattered. But to act on that finding, Google first had to figure out what its best managers did. So the researchers followed up with double-blind qualitative interviews, asking the high- and low-scoring managers questions such as "How often do you have career development discussions with your direct reports?" and "What do you do to develop a vision for your team?" Managers from Google's three major functions (engineering, global business, and general and administrative) participated; they came from all levels and geographies. The team also studied thousands of qualitative comments from Googlegeist surveys, performance reviews, and submissions for the company's Great Manager Award. (Each year, Google selects about 20 managers for this distinction, on the basis of employees' nominations.) It took several months to code and process all this information.

After much review, Oxygen identified eight behaviors shared by high-scoring managers. (See the sidebar "What Google's Best Managers Do" for the complete list.) Even though the behaviors weren't terribly surprising, Patel's colead, Michelle Donovan, says, "we hoped that the list would resonate because it was based on Google data. The attributes were about us, by us, and for us."

The key behaviors primarily describe leaders of small and medium-sized groups and teams and are especially relevant to first- and second-level managers. They involve developing and motivating direct reports, as well as communicating strategy and eliminating roadblocks—all vital activities that people tend to overlook in the press of their day-to-day responsibilities.

Putting the Findings into Practice

The list of behaviors has served three important functions at Google: giving employees a shared vocabulary for discussing management, offering them straightforward guidelines for improving it, and encapsulating the full range of management responsibilities. Though the list is simple and straightforward, it's enriched by examples and descriptions of best practices—in survey participants' own words. These details make the overarching principles, such as "empowers the team and does not micromanage," more concrete and show managers different ways of enacting them. (See the exhibit "How Google defines one key behavior.")

What Google's Best Managers Do

BY EXAMINING DATA from employee surveys and performance reviews, Google's people analytics team identified eight key behaviors demonstrated by the company's most effective managers.

A good manager:

1. Is a good coach

2. Empowers the team and does not micromanage

3. Expresses interest in and concern for team members' success and personal well-being

4. Is productive and results-oriented

5. Is a good communicator—listens and shares information

6. Helps with career development

7. Has a clear vision and strategy for the team

8. Has key technical skills that help him or her advise the team

The descriptions of the eight behaviors also allow considerable tailoring. They're inclusive guidelines, not rigid formulas. That said, it was clear early on that managers would need help adopting the new standards, so people ops built assessments and a training program around the Oxygen findings.

To improve the odds of acceptance, the group customized the survey instrument, creating an upward feedback survey (UFS) for employees in administrative and global business functions and a tech managers survey (TMS) for the engineers. Both assessments asked employees to evaluate their managers (using a five-point scale) on a core set of activities—such as giving actionable feedback regularly and communicating team goals clearly—all of which related directly to the key management behaviors.

The first surveys went out in June 2010—deliberately out of sync with performance reviews, which took place in April and September. (Google had initially considered linking the scores with performance reviews but decided that would increase resistance to the Oxygen program because employees would view it as a top-down

How Google defines one key behavior

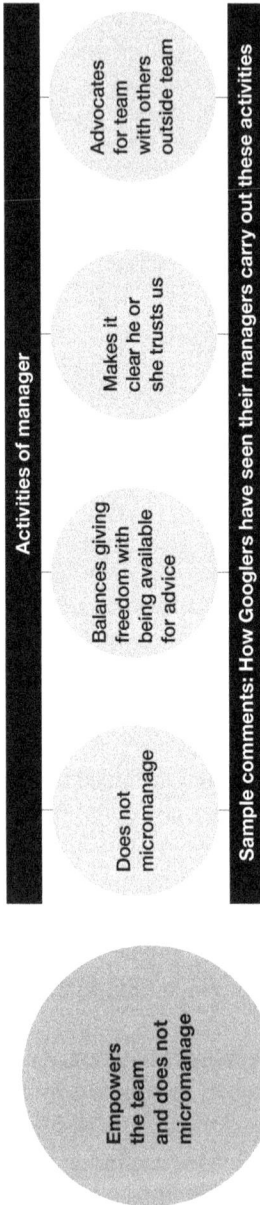

Empowers the team and does not micromanage

Drawing on companywide survey responses, Google breaks down each essential management behavior into specific activities and best practices.

Activities of manager

Does not micromanage

Balances giving freedom with being available for advice

Makes it clear he or she trusts us

Advocates for team with others outside team

Sample comments: How Googlers have seen their managers carry out these activities

"He doesn't micromanage me, is very logical, and is willing to listen to you and not run an evil agenda. He is very respectful...I would not think about leaving Google as long as he is my manager."

"When I worked for her, she gave me space to work independently, but she was there to support me when I encountered roadblocks or needed advice."

"He encourages people to run with ideas but knows when to step in and offer advice not to pursue a failing issue."

"She cultivates a culture of accountability while not losing sight of the fact that we can enjoy work. She knows she hired an excellent team, and she shares the fact that she trusts us."

"He is always advocating [for] me and the work I do. For example, when I designed a new feature, he encouraged me to present the feature at an all-hands [department-wide] meeting."

Best Practice: Assign stretch assignments to empower the team to tackle big problems

"My manager was able to see my potential and gave me opportunities that allowed me to shine and grow. For example, early on in my role, she asked me to pull together a cross-functional team to develop a goal-setting process. I was new to the role, so she figured it would be a great way for me to get to know the team and also to create accountability and transparency. Once it was developed, she sent me to one of our Europe offices—on my own!—to deliver the training to people managers there."

Source: The Google Internal Presentation "Investigating Why Managers Matter and What Our Best Ones Do," January 2010

imposition of standards.) People ops emphasized confidentiality and issued frequent reminders that the surveys were strictly for self-improvement. "Project Oxygen was always meant to be a developmental tool, not a performance metric," says Mary Kate Stimmler, an analyst in the department. "We realized that anonymous surveys are not always fair, and there is often a context behind low scores."

Though the surveys weren't mandatory, the vast majority of employees completed them. Soon afterward, managers received reports with numerical scores and individual comments—feedback they were urged to share with their teams. (See the sidebar "One Manager's Feedback" for a representative sample.) The reports explicitly tied individuals' scores to the eight behaviors, included links to more information about best practices, and suggested actions each manager could take to improve. Someone with, say, unfavorable scores in coaching might get a recommendation to take a class on how to deliver personalized, balanced feedback.

People ops designed the training to be hands-on and immediately useful. In "vision" classes, for example, participants practiced writing vision statements for their departments or teams and bringing the ideas to life with compelling stories. In 2011, Google added Start Right, a two-hour workshop for new managers, and Manager Flagship courses on popular topics such as managing change, which were offered in three two-day modules over six months. "We have a team of instructors," says people-development manager Kathrin O'Sullivan, "and we are piloting online Google Hangout classes so managers from around the world can participate."

Managers have expressed few concerns about signing up for the courses and going public with the changes they need to make. Eric Clayberg, for one, has found his training invaluable. A seasoned software-engineering manager and serial entrepreneur, Clayberg had led teams for 18 years before Google bought his latest start-up. But he feels he learned more about management in six months of Oxygen surveys and people ops courses than in the previous two decades. "For instance," he says, "I was worried about the flat organizational structure at Google; I knew it would be hard to help people on my team get promoted. I learned in the classes about how

One Manager's Feedback

GOOGLE MANAGERS RECEIVE SEMIANNUAL FEEDBACK REPORTS like this fictitious sample. Their employees rate them on a range of activities demonstrating key behaviors that the company has identified through empirical analysis. Each manager gets detailed pointers on applying the feedback and developing essential skills—practical guidance that traditional 360s generally lack.

Detailed results for "Jane Googler"

Here are the survey results for Googlers who reported directly to you as of 6/30/2012. We display the current items where three or more people responded.

Overall percent favorable: 95%

Top quartile for global team overall: 92%

Bottom quartile for global team overall: 73%

▨ % Favorable—the percentage of Googlers who selected "agree"/"strongly agree"

☐ % Neutral—the percentage of Googlers who selected "neutral"

▨ % Unfavorable—the percentage of Googlers who selected "disagree"/"strongly disagree"

N = number of responses

Item % favorable		vs Prior fav		vs Global team fav	N
		Q3- 2011	Q1- 2012		
1. My manager delivers difficult feedback constructively. 100		+8	—	+23	7
2. My manager gives me actionable feedback that helps me improve my performance. 100		+23	0	+25	8
19. My manager does not micromanage (get involved in details that should be handled at other levels). 88	12	+3	-12	+6	8
20. My manager regularly shares relevant information from his/her manager and senior leadership. 88	12	+11	+8	+5	8
21. My manager helps me understand how my work impacts the organization. 88	12	+3	—	+14	8

Item % favorable	vs Prior fav		vs Global team fav	N
	Q3-2011	Q1-2012		
22. My manager has regular 1:1s 88 / 12	+42	—	+3	8
23. My manager has the technical expertise required to effectively manage me. 86 / 14	—	+46	+8	7
24. My manager talks about all aspects of career development—not just promotions. 71 / 15 / 14	+7	—	+2	7
25. My manager has had a meaningful discussion with me about my career development in the past six months. 71 / 15 / 14	—	+31	–2	7

Comments

Here are the comments from Googlers who reported directly to you as of 6/30/2012. Please keep these comments **confidential.**

What would you recommend your manager keep doing?

- "Jane is extremely supportive and places trust in us as a team. This enables us to move quickly."

- "She's a fantastic people manager and gets the pulse of the team. She tackles tough situations with a calm and earnest manner."

- "She gives us a clear vision for the team. We know the biggest priorities ahead."

What would you have your manager change?

- "We have great general 1:1s, but it would be great to have dedicated career development discussions."

- "Jane can work on improving her process knowledge so she can talk over the more nitty-gritty details and decisions."

(continued)

One Manager's Feedback

(continued)

- "Jane is naturally soft-spoken and will need to be a bit more vocal when in disagreements. She's not always vocal right away, and with the challenges our team faces, we'll need to be strong in our opinions."
- "She could give us additional career development thoughts."

Taking Action

Here's how you can best use this report and communicate to your team that you've heard their feedback and will work with them on any improvement areas:

Share these results with your team

- Discuss your results at the next team meeting, and thank people for their feedback.
- Please remember that the survey is confidential, so it's important to talk about your overall feedback instead of trying to determine which of your

---

to provide career development beyond promotions. I now spend a third to half my time looking for ways to help my team members grow." And to his surprise, his reports have welcomed his advice. "Engineers hate being micromanaged on the technical side," he observes, "but they love being closely managed on the career side."

To complement the training, the development team sets up panel discussions featuring high-scoring managers from each function. That way, employees get advice from colleagues they respect, not just from HR. People ops also sends new managers automated e-mail reminders with tips on how to succeed at Google, links to relevant Oxygen findings, and information about courses they haven't taken.

And Google rewards the behaviors it's working so hard to promote. The company has revamped its selection criteria for the Great Manager Award to reflect the eight Oxygen behaviors. Employees refer to the behaviors and cite specific examples when submitting nominations. Clayberg has received the award, and he believes it was largely because of the skills he acquired through his Oxygen reports said what. Focus on reflecting on your overall results, including your identified strengths and areas for improvement.

Identify 1–2 attributes where you scored high

- Make sure you keep doing what you're doing here! Your strengths are just as important as your areas for improvement.
- Talk with your team to determine how to continue this performance and emphasize your strengths further.

Identify 1–2 attributes you would like to improve

- Establish your goals and—working with your team—put in place actions for improvement. Monitor your progress.
- Visit goto/managers for resources and guidance and tips from Great Manager Award winners to help you become the awesome manager that your team deserves.

training. The prize includes a weeklong trip to a destination such as Hawaii, where winners get to spend time with senior executives. Recipients go places in the company, too. "In the last round of promotions to vice president," Laszlo Bock says, "10% of the directors promoted were winners of the Great Manager Award."

Measuring Results

The people ops team has analyzed Oxygen's impact by examining aggregate survey data and qualitative input from individuals. From 2010 through 2012, UFS and TMS median favorability scores rose from 83% to 88%. The lowest-scoring managers improved the most, particularly in the areas of coaching and career development. The improvements were consistent across functions, survey categories, management levels, spans of control, and geographic regions.

In an environment of top achievers, people take low scores seriously. Consider vice president Sebastien Marotte, who came to Google in 2011 from a senior sales role at Oracle. During his first six months at Google, Marotte focused on meeting his sales numbers (and did so successfully) while managing a global team of 150 people. Then he received his first UFS scores, which came as a shock. "I asked myself, 'Am I right for this company? Should I go back to Oracle?' There seemed to be a disconnect," he says, "because my manager had rated me favorably in my first performance review, yet my UFS scores were terrible." Then, with help from a people ops colleague, Marotte took a step back and thought about what changes he could make. He recalls, "We went through all the comments and came up with a plan. I fixed how I communicated with my team and provided more visibility on our long-term strategy. Within two survey cycles, I raised my favorability ratings from 46% to 86%. It's been tough but very rewarding. I came here as a senior sales guy, but now I feel like a general manager."

Overall, other managers took the feedback as constructively as Marotte did—and were especially grateful for its specificity. Here's what Stephanie Davis, director of large-company sales and another winner of the Great Manager Award, says she learned from her first feedback report: "I was surprised that one person on my team didn't think I had regularly scheduled one-on-one meetings. I saw this person every day, but the survey helped me realize that just seeing this person was different from having regularly scheduled individual meetings. My team also wanted me to spend more time sharing my vision. Personally, I have always been inspired by Eric [Schmidt], Larry, and Sergey; I thought my team was also getting a sense of the company's vision from them. But this survey gave my team the opportunity to explain that they wanted me to interpret the higher-level vision for them. So I started listening to the company's earnings call with a different ear. I didn't just come back to my team with what was said; I also shared what it meant for them."

Chris Loux, head of global enterprise renewals, remembers feeling frustrated with his low UFS scores. "I had received a performance review indicating that I was exceeding expectations," he says, "yet one of my direct reports said on the UFS that he would not recommend me as a manager. That struck me, because people don't quit companies—they quit managers." At the same time, Loux struggled with the question of just how much to push the lower performers on his team. "It's hard to give negative feedback to a type-A person who has never received bad feedback in his or her life," he explains. "If someone gets 95% favorable on the UFS, I wonder if that manager is avoiding problems by not having tough conversations with reports on how they can get better."

Loux isn't the only Google executive to speculate about the connection between employees' performance reviews and their managers' feedback scores. That question came up multiple times during Oxygen's rollout. To address it, the people analytics group fell back on a time-tested technique—going back to the data and conducting a formal analysis to determine whether a manager who gave someone a negative performance review would then receive a low feedback rating from that employee. After looking at two quarters' worth of survey data from 2011, the group found that changes in employee performance ratings (both upward and downward) accounted for less than 1% of variability in corresponding manager ratings across all functions at Google.

"Managing to the test" doesn't appear to be a big risk, either. Because the eight behaviors are rooted in action, it's difficult for managers to fake them in pursuit of higher ratings. In the surveys, employees don't assess their managers' motivations, values, or beliefs; rather, they evaluate the extent to which their managers demonstrate each behavior. Either the manager has acted in the ways recommended—consistently and credibly—or she has not. There is very little room for grandstanding or dissembling.

"We are not trying to change the nature of people who work at Google," says Bock. "That would be presumptuous and dangerous. Instead, we are saying, 'Here are a few things that will lead you to be perceived as a better manager.' Our managers may not completely believe in the suggestions, but after they act on them and get better UFS and TMS scores, they may eventually internalize the behavior."

Project Oxygen does have its limits. A commitment to managerial excellence can be hard to maintain over the long haul. One threat to sustainability is "evaluation overload." The UFS and the TMS depend on employees' goodwill. Googlers voluntarily respond on a semiannual basis, but they're asked to complete many other surveys as well. What if they decide that they're tired of filling out surveys? Will response rates bottom out? Sustainability also depends on the continued effectiveness of managers who excel at the eight behaviors, as well as those behaviors' relevance to senior executive positions. A disproportionate number of recently promoted vice presidents had won the Great Manager Award, a reflection of how well they'd followed Oxygen's guidelines. But what if other behaviors—those associated with leadership skills—matter more in senior positions?

Further, while survey scores gauge employees' satisfaction and perceptions of the work environment, it's unclear exactly what impact those intangibles have on such bottom-line measures as sales, productivity, and profitability. (Even for Google's high-powered statisticians, those causal relationships are difficult to establish.) And if the eight behaviors do actually benefit organizational performance, they still might not give Google a lasting edge. Companies with similar competitive profiles—high-tech firms, for example, that are equally data-driven—can mimic Google's approach, since the eight behaviors aren't proprietary.

Still, Project Oxygen has accomplished what it set out to do: It not only convinced its skeptical audience of Googlers that managers mattered but also identified, described, and institutionalized their most essential behaviors. Oxygen applied the concept of data-driven continuous improvement directly—and successfully—to the soft skills of management. Widespread adoption has had a significant impact on how employees perceive life at Google—particularly on how they rate the degree of collaboration, the transparency of performance evaluations, and their groups' commitment to innovation and risk taking.

———————

At a company like Google, where the staff consists almost entirely of "A" players, managers have a complex, demanding role to play.

They must go beyond overseeing the day-to-day work and support their employees' personal needs, development, and career planning. That means providing smart, steady feedback to guide people to greater levels of achievement—but intervening judiciously and with a light touch, since high-performing knowledge workers place a premium on autonomy. It's a delicate balancing act to keep employees happy and motivated through enthusiastic cheerleading while helping them grow through stretch assignments and carefully modulated feedback. When the process works well, it can yield extraordinary results.

That's why Prasad Setty wants to keep building on Oxygen's findings about effective management practice. "We will have to start thinking about what else drives people to go from good to great," he says. His team has begun analyzing managers' assessment scores by personality type, looking for patterns. "With Project Oxygen, we didn't have these endogenous variables available to us," he adds. "Now we can start to tease them out, using more of an ethnographic approach. It's really about observations—staying with people and studying their interactions. We're not going to have the capacity to follow tons of people, but what we'll lose in terms of numbers, we'll gain in a deeper understanding of what managers and their teams experience."

That, in a nutshell, is the principle at the heart of Google's approach: deploying disciplined data collection and rigorous analysis—the tools of science—to uncover deeper insights into the art and craft of management.

Originally published in December 2013. Reprint R1312D

21st-Century Talent Spotting

by Claudio Fernández-Aráoz

A FEW YEARS AGO, I was asked to help find a new CEO for a family-owned electronics retailer that wanted to professionalize its management and expand its operations. I worked closely with the outgoing chief executive and the board to pinpoint the relevant competencies for the job and then seek out and assess candidates. The man we hired had all the right credentials: He'd attended top professional schools and worked for some of the best organizations in the industry, and he was a successful country manager in one of the world's most admired companies. Even more important, he'd scored above the target level for each of the competencies we'd identified. But none of that mattered. Despite his impressive background and great fit, he could not adjust to the massive technological, competitive, and regulatory changes occurring in the market at the time. Following three years of lackluster performance, he was asked to leave.

Compare that story with one from the start of my executive search career. My task was to fill a project manager role at a small brewery owned by Quinsa, which then dominated the beer market in the southern cone of Latin America. In those days, I hadn't yet heard the term "competency." I was working in a new office without research support (in the pre-internet era), and Quinsa was the only serious beverage industry player in the region, so I was simply unable to identify a large pool of people with the right industry and functional background. Ultimately, I contacted Pedro Algorta, an executive I'd met in 1981, while we were both studying at Stanford University. A survivor of the infamous 1972 plane crash in the Andes, which has been chronicled in several books and the movie *Alive*, Algorta was certainly an interesting choice. But he had no experience in the consumer goods business; was unfamiliar with Corrientes, the province where the brewery was located; and had never worked in marketing or sales, key areas of expertise. Still, I had a feeling he would be successful, and Quinsa agreed to hire him. That decision proved to be a smart one. Algorta was rapidly promoted to general manager of the Corrientes brewery and then CEO of Quinsa's flagship Quilmes brewery. He also became a key member of the team that transformed Quinsa from a family-owned enterprise to a large, respected conglomerate with a management team considered at the time to be among the best in Latin America.

Why did the CEO of the electronics business, who seemed so right for the position, fail so miserably? And why did Algorta, so clearly unqualified, succeed so spectacularly? The answer is *potential:* the ability to adapt to and grow into increasingly complex roles and environments. Algorta had it; the first CEO did not.

Having spent 30 years evaluating and tracking executives and studying the factors in their performance, I now consider potential to be the most important predictor of success at all levels, from junior management to the C-suite and the board. I've learned how to identify people who have it and to help companies develop and deploy them. With this article, I share those lessons. As business becomes more volatile and complex, and the global market for top professionals gets tighter, I am convinced that organizations and their leaders must transition to what I think of as a new era of talent spotting—one in which our evaluations of one another are based not on brawn, brains, experience, or competencies, but on potential.

A New Era

The first era of talent spotting lasted millennia. For thousands of years, humans made choices about one another on the basis of

Idea in Brief

The Problem

In the past few decades, organizations have emphasized "competencies" in hiring and developing talent. Jobs have been decomposed into skills and filled by candidates who have them. But 21st-century business is too volatile and complex—and the market for top talent too tight—for that model to work anymore.

The Solution

Today those responsible for hiring and promotion decisions

must instead focus on potential: the ability to adapt to ever-changing business environments and grow into challenging new roles.

The Tools

Managers must learn to assess current and prospective employees on five key indicators: the right motivation, curiosity, insight, engagement, and determination. Then they have to help the best get better with smart retention and stretch assignments.

physical attributes. If you wanted to erect a pyramid, dig a canal, fight a war, or harvest a crop, you chose the fittest, healthiest, strongest people you could find. Those attributes were easy to assess, and, despite their growing irrelevance, we still unconsciously look for them: *Fortune* 500 CEOs are on average 2.5 inches taller than the average American, and the statistics on military leaders and country presidents are similar.

I was born and raised during the second era, which emphasized intelligence, experience, and past performance. Throughout much of the 20th century, IQ—verbal, analytical, mathematical, and logical cleverness—was justifiably seen as an important factor in hiring processes (particularly for white-collar roles), with educational pedigrees and tests used as proxies. Much work also became standardized and professionalized. Many kinds of workers could be certified with reliability and transparency, and since most roles were relatively similar across companies and industries, and from year to year, past performance was considered a fine indicator. If you were looking for an engineer, accountant, lawyer, designer, or CEO, you would scout out, interview, and hire the smartest, most experienced engineer, accountant, lawyer, designer, or CEO.

I joined the executive search profession in the 1980s, at the beginning of the third era of talent spotting, which was driven by the competency movement still prevalent today. David McClelland's 1973 paper "Testing for Competence Rather than for 'Intelligence'" proposed that workers, especially managers, be evaluated on specific characteristics and skills that helped predict outstanding performance in the roles for which they were being hired. The time was right for such thinking, because technological evolution and industry convergence had made jobs much more complex, often rendering experience and performance in previous positions irrelevant. So, instead, we decomposed jobs into competencies and looked for candidates with the right combination of them. For leadership roles, we also began to rely on research showing that emotional intelligence was even more important than IQ.

Now we're at the dawn of a fourth era, in which the focus must shift to potential. In a volatile, uncertain, complex, and ambiguous environment (VUCA is the military-acronym-turned-corporate-buzzword), competency-based appraisals and appointments are increasingly insufficient. What makes someone successful in a particular role today might not tomorrow if the competitive environment shifts, the company's strategy changes, or he or she must collaborate with or manage a different group of colleagues. So the question is not whether your company's employees and leaders have the right skills; it's whether they have the potential to learn new ones.

The Scarcity of Top Talent

Unfortunately, potential is much harder to discern than competence (though not impossible, as I'll describe later). Moreover, your organization will be looking for it in what will soon be one of the toughest employment markets in history—for employers, not job seekers. The recent noise about high unemployment rates in the United States and Europe hides important signals: Three forces—globalization, demographics, and pipelines—will make senior talent ever scarcer in the years to come.

Back in 2006, I worked with Nitin Nohria, the current dean of Harvard Business School, and my Egon Zehnder colleagues to study this issue, gathering detailed data and interviewing CEOs from 47 companies with a combined market capitalization of $2 trillion, revenue of over $1 trillion, and more than 3 million employees. Representing all major sectors and geographies, these firms were successful, with strong reputations and solid people practices. Yet we found that all were about to face a massive talent crunch. Eight years later, the situation for companies is just as bad, if not worse.

Let's examine the three factors in turn. *Globalization* compels companies to reach beyond their home markets and to compete for the people who can help them do so. The major global firms in our 2006 study anticipated an 88% increase in their proportion of revenue from developing regions by 2012. Not only did that happen, but the International Monetary Fund and other groups are currently predicting that some 70% of the world's growth between now and 2016 will come from emerging markets. At the same time, firms in developing nations are themselves vying for talent, as well as customers, around the world. Take China, which now has 88 companies in the global *Fortune* 500, up from just eight in 2003, thanks in part to foreign growth. Huawei, the leading Chinese telecommunications company, employs more than 70,000 people, 45% of whom work in R&D centers in countries including Germany, Sweden, the U.S., France, Italy, Russia, and India. Similar examples can be found in companies based in markets such as India and Brazil.

The impact of *demographics* on hiring pools is also undeniable. The sweet spot for rising senior executives is the 35-to-44-year-old age bracket, but the percentage of people in that range is shrinking dramatically. In our 2006 study, we calculated that a projected 30% decline in the ranks of young leaders, combined with anticipated business growth, would cut in half the pool of senior leader candidates in that critical age group. Whereas a decade ago this demographic shift was affecting mostly the United States and Europe, by 2020 many other countries, including Russia, Canada, South Korea, and China, will have more people at retirement age than entering the workforce.

Potential at the Top

A FOCUS ON POTENTIAL can improve talent spotting at every level of the organization—especially the very top. When choosing a CEO or board member, as opposed to a young manager, you'll often find that several candidates have the right credentials, experience, and competencies. That's why an accurate assessment of their motivation, curiosity, insight, engagement, and determination is all the more important.

For CEO roles, succession planning must start very early, ideally when a new leader takes charge but no later than three to four years before he or she expects to leave. At Egon Zehnder, even when a much longer tenure is expected, we help companies assess potential two to four layers below the C-suite, identifying people to retain and develop so that some can become contenders for the top job.

I know one outstanding corporate director who twice orchestrated the dismissal of fully competent C-suite executives because they didn't have enough potential and she wanted to make their roles—key development opportunities—available to people who did. Board appointments require the same discipline. Our firm's UK office recently helped a highly respected retail group, the John Lewis Partnership, evaluate a long list of candidates for two nonexecutive director positions, using all the indicators of potential—curiosity, in particular—as key metrics. After all, if a company's leaders don't have the potential to learn, grow, and adapt to new environments, how can they attract up-and-coming employees and managers who do?

The third phenomenon is related and equally powerful, but much less well known: Companies are not properly developing their *pipelines* of future leaders. In PricewaterhouseCoopers's 2014 survey of CEOs in 68 countries, 63% of respondents said they were concerned about the future availability of key skills at all levels. The Boston Consulting Group cites proprietary research showing that 56% of executives see critical gaps in their ability to fill senior managerial roles in coming years. HBS professor Boris Groysberg found similar concerns in his 2013 survey of executive program participants: Respondents gave their companies' leadership pipelines an average rating of 3.2 out of 5, compared with an average score of 4 for current CEOs and 3.8 for current top teams. Equally troubling were responses to other kinds of questions in the survey: No talent management function was rated higher than 3.3, and critical employee development activities, such as job rotations, were scored as low as 2.6. In other words, few executives think their companies are doing a good job identifying and developing qualified leaders. Recent executive panel interviews conducted by my colleagues confirm that this view is widespread. Only 22% of the 823 leaders who participated consider their pipelines promising, and only 19% said they find it easy to attract the best talent.

In many companies, particularly those based in developed markets, I've found that half of senior leaders will be eligible for retirement within the next two years, and half of them don't have a successor ready or able to take over. As Groysberg puts it, "Companies may not be feeling pain today, but in five or 10 years, as people retire or move on, where will the next generation of leaders come from?"

Taken independently, globalization, demographics, and pipelines would each create unprecedented demand for talent over the next decade. The pace of globalization has never been faster; the imbalance between old and young has never been so dramatic; views on the pipelines of qualified successors have never been more negative; and the survey ratings of development practices are the lowest I've seen. Combine all those factors, and you get a war for talent that will present a huge, perhaps insurmountable, challenge for most organizations. But for those that learn how to spot potential, effectively retain people who have it, and create development programs to help the best get better, the situation will instead offer an extraordinary opportunity.

Better Hiring

The first step is to get the right people into your organization. As Amazon CEO Jeff Bezos, one of the most impressive corporate value creators in recent history, put it in 1998, "Setting the bar high in our approach to hiring has been, and will continue to be, the single most important element of [our] success." So, when evaluating job candidates (and reevaluating current employees), how do you gauge potential?

Many companies have well-established "high potential" programs, through which they fast-track promising managers for development and promotions. But most of these are actually "high performer" programs, full of people who have done well in the past and are therefore assumed to have the best shot of doing well in the future—but given VUCA conditions, that is no longer a safe prediction. About 80% of the participants in the executive programs I teach consistently report that their companies don't use an empirically validated model for assessing potential. I'll admit, this kind of evaluation is much more difficult than measuring IQ, past performance, and even various competencies. But it can be done—with a predictive accuracy around 85%, according to data on the careers of thousands of executives we assessed at Egon Zehnder using a model developed and refined over the past two decades.

The first indicator of potential we look for is the right kind of *motivation:* a fierce commitment to excel in the pursuit of unselfish goals. High potentials have great ambition and want to leave their mark, but they also aspire to big, collective goals, show deep personal humility, and invest in getting better at everything they do. We consider motivation first because it is a stable—and usually unconscious—quality. If someone is driven purely by selfish motives, that probably won't change.

We then consider four other qualities that are hallmarks of potential, according to our research:

- **Curiosity:** a penchant for seeking out new experiences, knowledge, and candid feedback and an openness to learning and change

- **Insight:** the ability to gather and make sense of information that suggests new possibilities

- **Engagement:** a knack for using emotion and logic to communicate a persuasive vision and connect with people

- **Determination:** the wherewithal to fight for difficult goals despite challenges and to bounce back from adversity

In retrospect, I can see that Pedro Algorta succeeded at Quinsa because he had all those qualities, not because he possessed a specific set of skills and competencies. And those qualities were in high relief during his harrowing ordeal in the Andes. He demonstrated his motivation by playing a critical yet humble role—providing sustenance for the explorers who would eventually march out to save the group. He melted snow for them to drink and cut and dried small pieces of flesh from the dead bodies of fellow victims to serve as food. Instead of succumbing to despair, Algorta became curious about the environment around him, taking an interest in the water coming off the ice. It flowed east, leading him, and only him, to the insight that the dying pilot had misreported their position; they were on the Argentine side of the mountain range, not on the Chilean side. His engagement and determination were also clear over those 72 days. He faithfully tended to his dying friend, Arturo Nogueira, who had suffered multiple leg fractures, trying to distract the young man from his pain. He encouraged his fellow survivors to maintain hope and persuaded them all to condone the consumption of their own bodies, should they die, describing it as "an act of love."

Although Algorta's tenure as CEO bears no resemblance to what he experienced on that mountain, the same characteristics served him in his career at Quinsa. Perhaps the best example of the purity of his motives came at the end of his 10-year stint with the company, when, for sound strategic reasons, he recommended that it abandon the agribusiness project he was leading, thus voting himself out of a job. He was also a curious executive, always going out of his way to meet customers, clients, and workers at all levels, and to listen to voices that usually went unheard. As a result, he accepted and supported some revolutionary marketing initiatives, which allowed Quilmes to multiply its sales eightfold while achieving record profitability. He displayed great insight both in his hiring decisions—the future CEOs of both Quilmes and Nestlé were among his best hires—and in his strategic ones: for example, his bold move to divest all noncore assets so that the company could use the proceeds to expand the regional brewery business. His engagement transformed an ineffective and even vicious culture at Quilmes; his insistence that bosses and subordinates come together in open meetings set a precedent that was later rolled out to the whole group. Finally, Algorta showed amazing determination at Quinsa. When the project he'd been hired to lead—the construction of a new brewery—ran out of funds just after he took over, he didn't consider quitting; instead, he pushed to get the necessary financing. And when Argentina was shaken by devaluation and hyperinflation a few months later, he pressed on; the facility was up and running in 15 months.

How can you tell if a candidate you've just met—or a current employee—has potential? By mining his or her personal and professional history, as I've just done with Algorta's. Conduct in-depth interviews or career discussions, and do thorough reference checks to uncover stories that demonstrate whether the person has (or lacks) these qualities. For instance, to assess curiosity, don't just ask, "Are you curious?" Instead, look for signs that the person believes in self-improvement, truly enjoys learning, and is able to recalibrate after missteps. Questions like the following can help:

- How do you react when someone challenges you?

- How do you invite input from others on your team?

- What do you do to broaden your thinking, experience, or personal development?

- How do you foster learning in your organization?

- What steps do you take to seek out the unknown?

Always ask for concrete examples, and go just as deep in your exploration of motivation, insight, engagement, and determination. Your conversations with managers, colleagues, and direct reports who know the person well should be just as detailed.

As a leader, you must also work to spread these interviewing techniques through the organization. Researchers have found that while the best interviewers' assessments have a very high positive correlation with the candidates' ultimate performance, some interviewers' opinions are worse than flipping a coin. Still, few managers learn proper assessment techniques from their business schools or their employers; in my surveys of participants in executive talent management programs, I've found that only about 30% think that their companies provide adequate training. Most organizations, it seems, are filled with people who have the power to endorse bad candidates and kill off good ones.

By contrast, companies that emphasize the right kind of hiring vastly improve their odds. Amazon has, for example, hundreds of dedicated internal recruiters, great training programs in assessment, and even a legion of certified "bar raisers": skilled evaluators who hold full-time jobs in a range of departments but are also empowered to participate in assessing—and vetoing—candidates for other areas.

The Brazilian mining group Companhia Vale do Rio Doce, known as Vale, took a similarly disciplined approach, working with Egon Zehnder, during the 2001 to 2011 tenure of CEO Roger Agnelli. On his watch, not one senior role was filled without an objective, independent, and professional assessment of all internal and external candidates. Managers were encouraged to favor motivated, curious, insightful, engaging, and determined prospects even when they had no specific experience in the field or function to which they had applied. "We would never choose someone who was not passionate and committed to our long-term strategy and demanding objectives," Agnelli explains. Some 250 executives were hired or promoted in this way, all over the world, and the strategy paid off. Vale became a global player in the mining industry, dramatically outperforming others in the country and the region.

Smart Retention

Once you've hired true high potentials and identified the ones you already have, you'll need to focus on keeping them. After all, competitors grappling with the same tight talent market will be more than happy to tempt them away. Agnelli says his proudest achievement at Vale was not the huge revenue, profit, and share price growth over which he presided but the improved quality of the leaders rising through the company's ranks. "After five or six years, everyone appointed at the highest levels came from inside," he says, adding that the capacity to build and retain great teams is *"the* key" to any leader's or organization's success.

Indeed, when the Brazilian government used its 61% stake in Vale's controlling shares to precipitate Agnelli's departure, in 2011, prompting the voluntary resignations of seven out of eight executive committee members within a year, the company soon lost almost half its value. Growing disenchantment with Brazilian and commodity stocks played a role, to be sure. But given that Vale's closest competitors, Rio Tinto and BHP Billiton, saw much less dramatic declines over the same period, it seems clear that investors were also reacting to the loss of an outstanding leadership team.

How can you emulate Vale under Agnelli and avoid the company's subsequent fate? By considering what your high potentials want most from you. As Daniel H. Pink explains in *Drive,* most of us (especially knowledge workers) are energized by three fundamental things: *autonomy*—the freedom to direct our lives; *mastery*—our craving to excel; and *purpose*—the yearning for our work to serve something larger than ourselves.

Pay does matter, of course. All employees, especially rising stars, expect their compensation to reflect their contribution or effort and to be comparable to that of others doing similar jobs. However, in my experience, while unfair pay can surely demotivate, compensation beyond a certain level is much less important than most people think. In my examination of candidates hired through our firm who were successful in their new jobs but moved on within three years, I found that 85% of them were hired away into a more senior position, confirming that they were competent people with potential. But only 4% of them cited more money as the primary reason for their departures. More common reasons were bad bosses, limited support, and lack of opportunities for growth.

So do pay your stars fairly, ideally above the average. But also give them autonomy in four "T" dimensions: task (what they do), time (when they do it), team (whom they do it with), and technique (how they do it). Help them toward mastery by setting difficult but attainable challenges and eliminating distractions. And engage them in a greater team, organizational, or societal goal. Bezos and other leaders at Amazon are expert at this. Agnelli and his team at Vale were, too. But the conditions at the company following his departure failed to motivate the remaining leaders in the same way, and many of them chose to move on.

Stretch Development

Your final job is to make sure your stars live up to the high potential you've spotted in them by offering development opportunities that push them out of their comfort zones. Jonathan Harvey, a top HR executive at ANZ, an Australian bank that operates in 33 countries, puts it this way: "When it comes to developing executives for future leadership assignments, we're constantly striving to find the optimal level of discomfort in the next role or project, because that's where the most learning happens. We don't want people to be stretched beyond their limits. But we want well-rounded, values-focused leaders who see the world through a wide-angle lens, and the right stretch assignments are what helps people get there."

To explain the consequences of *not* challenging your high potentials, I often point to Japan. In 2008 Kentaro Aramaki, from Egon Zehnder's Tokyo office, and I mapped the potential of senior Japanese executives (that is, our consultants' objective assessments of the executives' ability to take on bigger roles and responsibilities, as measured by the indicators described above) against their competence (that is, our objective assessments of the eight leadership competencies listed in the sidebar "What Else Should You Look For?"). When we compared those scores with the average scores of all executives in our worldwide database, we found a great paradox. Japanese professionals had higher potential than the global average but lower competence. In spite of great raw material, there was a poor final product. The problem was, and still is, Japan's flawed development process. Although the country's educational institutions and the strong work ethic that is part of Japanese culture give managers a jump-start in their careers, their growth is stymied when they actually start working. A leader in Japan traditionally rises through

What Else Should You Look For?

Although potential should be the defining measure of executives today, it would be a mistake to ignore other lessons we've learned over the years about how to evaluate people.

Intelligence

Although you probably won't administer an IQ test, it is important to assess a candidate's general intelligence (including analytical, verbal, mathematical, and logical reasoning) by considering educational background, early job experiences, and responses to interview questions. You don't need to look for geniuses; for most jobs anything above a certain level of intelligence has almost no impact on performance. However, you should still hire people clever enough for your requirements, because their general intelligence won't increase dramatically over time.

Values

Values are critical, and you can't expect to impart them on the job. Use interviews and reference checks not only to weigh the essentials, such as honesty and integrity, but also to discover if the candidate shares your organization's core values.

Leadership Abilities

Some competencies are relevant (though not sufficient) when evaluating senior manager candidates. While each job and organization is different, the best leaders have, in some measure, eight abilities.

---

the ranks of one division, in one company, waiting respectfully for promotions that usually come only when he's the most senior person in line for the spot.

Recently a Tokyo-based global conglomerate asked our firm to assess its top dozen senior leaders, all in their mid- to late 50s. This company, which operates in multiple industries and markets, should have been an ideal training ground for executives. However, only one of the managers we evaluated had worked in more than a single business line. The time each had spent working outside Japan was just one year, on average. And their English language skills were quite limited. As a result, none were suitable candidates to succeed the CEO. The

1. **Strategic orientation.** The capacity to engage in broad, complex analytical and conceptual thinking

2. **Market insight.** A strong understanding of the market and how it affects the business

3. **Results orientation.** A commitment to demonstrably improving key business metrics

4. **Customer impact.** A passion for serving the customer

5. **Collaboration and influence.** An ability to work effectively with peers or partners, including those not in the line of command

6. **Organizational development.** A drive to improve the company by attracting and developing top talent

7. **Team leadership.** Success in focusing, aligning, and building effective groups

8. **Change leadership.** The capacity to transform and align an organization around a new goal

You should assess these abilities through interviews and reference checks, in the same way you would evaluate potential, aiming to confirm that the candidate has displayed them in the past, under similar circumstances.

sad thing is that all had started off strong. They were engineers, with an average tenure of more than 20 years in R&D and product strategy and marketing—but that potential had been squandered.

Pushing your high potentials up a straight ladder toward bigger jobs, budgets, and staffs will continue their growth, but it won't accelerate it. Diverse, complex, challenging, uncomfortable roles will. When we recently asked 823 international executives to look back at their careers and tell us what had helped them unleash their potential, the most popular answer, cited by 71%, was stretch assignments. Job rotations and personal mentors, each mentioned by 49% of respondents, tied for second.

How do you make sure people in your organization are getting the stretch assignments and job rotations they need? Let's come back to ANZ. Following a 2007 to 2010 hiring spree as the company expanded across Asia, it decided to refine its leadership development processes. Its efforts center on what it calls business-critical roles: those that make a vital contribution to the strategic agenda; require a scarce set of skills; produce highly variable outcomes dependent on the incumbent; and, if vacant, pose a significant threat to business continuity and performance momentum.

ANZ makes a point of assessing all its managers for potential and then placing those who rate the highest in these business-critical roles. Other development initiatives include the Generalist Bankers Program, which each year offers 10 to 15 participants the opportunity to spend two years rotating through wholesale, commercial, and retail banking, risk, and operations to build broad industry and corporate knowledge. Participants then move into permanent roles with a focus on gaining geographic, cultural, product, and client-facing experience, including a mandatory posting in internal audit to ensure that they understand the bank's control frameworks. The program commitment is 15 years, with the goal of a country CEO posting at the end.

This disciplined approach already seems to be bearing fruit. Whereas three years ago 70% of ANZ's senior executive roles were filled by external candidates, outside hiring is now below 20%. Internal surveys show that staff engagement has increased from 64% to 72%, while "same-period performance excellence" (a measure of employee commitment to customer service and product quality) has jumped from 68% to 78%. And the business has benefited in other ways. In 2013 the company was judged the number four international bank in the Asia Pacific region for the second consecutive year by the highly regarded Greenwich customer survey, up from number 12 in 2008.

———————

Geopolitics, business, industries, and jobs are changing so rapidly that we can't predict the competencies needed to succeed even a few years out. It is therefore imperative to identify and develop people with the highest potential. Look for those who have a strong motivation to excel in the pursuit of challenging goals, along with the humility to put the group ahead of individual needs; an insatiable curiosity that propels them to explore new ideas and avenues; keen insight that allows them to see connections where others don't; a strong engagement with their work and the people around them; and the determination to overcome setbacks and obstacles. That doesn't mean forgetting about factors like intelligence, experience, performance, and specific competencies, particularly the ones related to leadership. But hiring for potential and effectively retaining and developing those who have it—at every level of the organization—should now be your top priority.

Originally published in June 2014. Reprint R1406B

About the Contributors

DEREK VAN BEVER, a senior lecturer at HBS, is the director of the Forum for Growth and Innovation and was a member of the founding executive team of the advisory firm CEB.

JULIAN BIRKINSHAW is a professor of strategy and entrepreneurship at the London Business School.

CHRIS BRAHM is a leader of Bain's Technology practice in the Americas and a partner in San Francisco.

GREGORY CAIMI is a partner in Bain's Technology and Organization practices based in San Francisco.

CLAYTON M. CHRISTENSEN is the Kim B. Clark Professor of Business Administration at Harvard Business School.

FRANK VAN DEN DRIEST is a founder of the global marketing strategy consultancy EffectiveBrands (now Millward Brown Vermeer) and the coauthor (with Marc de Swaan Arons) of *The Global Brand CEO* (Airstream New York, 2010).

CLAUDIO FERNÁNDEZ-ARÁOZ is a senior adviser at the global executive search firm Egon Zehnder and the author of *It's Not the How or the What but the Who* (Harvard Business Review Press, 2014), on which this article is based.

DAVID A. GARVIN is the C. Roland Christensen Professor of Business Administration at Harvard Business School.

DANIEL GOLEMAN, a codirector of the Consortium for Research on Emotional Intelligence in Organizations at Rutgers University, is the author of *Focus: The Hidden Driver of Excellence* (HarperCollins, 2013).

TARUN KHANNA is the Jorge Paulo Lemann Professor at Harvard Business School and the director of Harvard University's South Asia Institute.

W. CHAN KIM is professor of strategy and management at INSEAD and codirector of the INSEAD Blue Ocean Strategy Institute, in Fontainebleau, France. He is the coauthor (with Reneé Mauborgne) of *Blue Ocean Strategy* (Harvard Business Review Press, 2015).

MICHAEL MANKINS leads Bain's Organization practice in the Americas and is a partner in San Francisco. He is a coauthor (with Marcia W. Blenko and Paul Rogers) of *Decide & Deliver: Five Steps to Breakthrough Performance in Your Organization* (Harvard Business Review Press, 2010).

ROGER L. MARTIN is a professor and the former dean at the University of Toronto's Rotman School of Management. He is a coauthor (with A.G. Lafley) of *Playing to Win: How Strategy Really Works* (Harvard Business Review Press, 2013).

RENÉE MAUBORGNE is professor of strategy and management at INSEAD and codirector of the INSEAD Blue Ocean Strategy Institute, in Fontainebleau, France. She is the coauthor (with W. Chan Kim) of *Blue Ocean Strategy* (Harvard Business Review Press, 2015).

PATTY MCCORD is the founder of Patty McCord Consulting and the former chief talent officer at Netflix.

MARC DE SWAAN ARONS is a founder of the global marketing strategy consultancy EffectiveBrands (now Millward Brown Vermeer) and the coauthor (with Frank van den Driest) of *The Global Brand CEO* (Airstream New York, 2010).

KEITH WEED is the chief marketing and communication officer of Unilever and the chairman of the Marketing2020 advisory board.

Index

New Ideas and Resources to Help You Achieve Even More with
Harvard Business Review

EASIER, SMARTER, PERSONALIZED

As a business executive, you are called upon to lead; *Harvard Business Review* provides the tools to keep you ahead, including the beautifully redesigned HBR.org. Imagine …

- On-demand access to more than 4,000 articles, interviews, features, and ideas in HBR.org's reimagined archive.

- Just-published articles **on topics you choose** rushed to your personalized My Library

- Seamless sharing of content with your colleagues.

Now, don't just imagine it. Employ it!

The most important management ideas all in one place.

We hope you enjoyed this HBR's 10 Must Reads book. Now, you can get even more with HBR's 10 Must Reads Boxed Set. From books on leadership and strategy to managing yourself and others, this 6-book collection delivers articles on the most essential business topics to help you succeed.

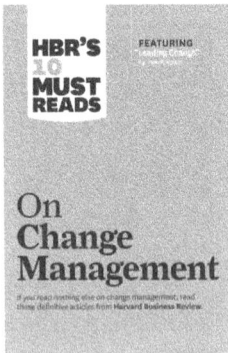

HBR's 10 Must Reads Series

The HBR's 10 Must Reads Series is the definitive collection of ideas and best practices on our most sought-after topics from the best minds in business.

- The Essentials
- Leadership
- Strategy
- Managing People
- Managing Yourself
- Collaboration
- Communication
- Making Smart Decisions
- Teams
- Innovation
- Strategic Marketing
- Change Management